The Southern Soldier Boy

The Southern Soldier Boy

The Experiences of a Confederate Soldier
of the 56th North Carolina Regiment
During the American Civil War

James Carson

LEONAUR

The Southern Soldier Boy: the Experiences of a Confederate Soldier
of the 56th North Carolina Regiment During the American Civil War
by James Carson

Leonaur is an imprint of Oakpast Ltd

ISBN: 978-0-85706-184-3 (hardcover)
ISBN: 978-0-85706-183-6 (softcover)

http://www.leonaur.com

Publisher's Note

The author of this book was from the Southern states of America and was engaged fighting for the Confederates during the American civil war. Like many of his compatriots he believed that the enslavement of negro men, women and children was part of the natural order of things ordained by God. In re-publishing this book it is not our intention to cause offence to anyone, but we do believe that the views expressed herein, which we do not share, provide essential historical context, and so they have been retained as the author wrote them.

Contents

Preface

A readable book should instruct, entertain and amuse. The author, outside of the historical interest of this little book, has aimed to cover a broad-enough field for all classes of readers to find some nourishing food—at least in the way of variety and shifting scenes—from the standpoint of a young private.

And in order to understand his viewpoint, a brief sketch of the author is admissible. Born in Cleveland County, N. C., about midway between Charlotte and Asheville, July 12, 1845. His father, a small slaveholder and a farmer, he was brought up to work on the farm and was well practiced in the use of firearms, and was well seasoned in the fox-chase and hunting sports. His father was an ardent Whig, and they got their political inspiration from William G. Brownlow's Knoxville, Tenn., Whig. (See Brownlow's and Pryneis' debate on Negro slavery.) Brownlow proved conclusively that slavery was of Divine origin; that it had always existed and always would exist, because the Bible said, "The heathen you buy with your money shall never go free, but shall be an inheritance to you and your children forever." But when hostilities began, Brownlow sided with the Union and was the war governor of Tennessee. The war spirit ran high in our section and all the boys were eager to take a hand in the fun of chasing the invaders out of our country. The first Manassas battle started them back the way our *smart men* said they would go. And I thought the fun would all be over before I would have a chance to share in the glory. But they kept coming in larger swarms. After I had organized and drilled with the Home Guards, I saw there was still a prospect to get to the front in time to take a hand. Two years had dragged along, the battle of Gettysburg had turned the scale, more than half of my early in friends had been knocked out when I entered the army for a three-years' term at the age of 18 years. We had understood at the first that we must fight three to one, but to whip that many Yankees was not thought to be much of a job; but when I waded in, it was quite evident that we must fight five to one. But we still thought they must be whipped, all the same. The numbers come up to our expectations, but we were sadly deceived in their fighting qualities. When they first came our climate did not agree with them, but the longer they stayed the harder they were to persuade away; and they finally worried us out, until we had to let them alone; and after staying with us awhile we learned they are as good as we are. From a distance, they are inclined to view us with a critic's eye, as through a glass darkly; but when they come down and bring their washing, they get a clearer view. Then, and not until then, the veil is removed away, and all our problems stand revealed in open day. Progress comes through evolution and revolution; where moral forces lag physical force compels the way. The only issue now is in patriotic rivalry of the sections. The heritage of one is the property of all.

Oh! Carry Me Back to Old Virginia, The Old Kentucky Home, Carolina, Oh, for Carolina, Away Down in Georgia, On the Sewanee River, etc., are refrains not equalled in the more frigid region. Then we have *Dixie*, covering the whole southland. All these are now held in common by our whole people. Whoever heard of any one ever wanting to be carried back to New England, where the natural resources are mainly ice, granite, rock, codfish and beans. Still we are all proud of the hardy New Englander who makes the desert blossom as the rose wherever he pitches his tent. His hard environment has been a blessing to every other part of the country, forcing him to seek greener pastures in balmier climes, and to disseminate his energy and frugality in those more leisurely sections that need encouragement to greater thrift. It was the combined qualities of the Virginia cavalier and the New England puritan that made Stonewall Jackson invincible and Robert E. Lee the highest type of the American patriot.

Jamestown and its Significance

The English settlement at Jamestown, Virginia, was the beginning of the highest civilization in the liberty of man and the establishment of the purest and best political government the world has ever known—perfected through many vicissitudes, stands as the beacon light of human liberty for all the world.

The Jamestown Exposition

The 26th of April, 1607, is the date that will linger in history after many a dreary record of battle and coronation has been swept away. For on that date the first permanent colony of English speech made its landing on the soil of North America. It is fitting that the three hundredth anniversary of this event should be marked by the opening of the Jamestown Exposition.

The founding of Jamestown was not a step in a struggle, but a trophy of victory. And, though it began the westward march of the Saxon tongue, which has long since encircled the globe, it marked the victory less of a race than of a civilization. It was really the dedication of a continent to individual liberty; it was the definite announcement that the worn-out systems of empire should not usurp the new western land. It was a trophy gained in a hundred years of such warfare as the world has rarely seen, but it was a thousand times worth the price.

When the peoples of Europe landed on the shores of the sixteenth century, they were a curiously assorted company. Germany was still playing the solemn farce of the Roman Empire, whose real existence had terminated a thousand years before. Spain had just driven the last armed infidel from her borders, and was preparing to use in foreign conquest the military excellence she had developed in her long crusade at home. Italy, divided into a dozen small states, had carried civilization as high as a purely city civilization can go, and was ready to decline. France was halting between two opinions, but, on the whole, leaned strongly toward the course of European aggression, which she pursued for centuries. All these countries were organized on the military plan. The individual counted for little among them; commerce counted for less; all who were not soldiers could escape contempt only by becoming priests. In England and Holland a different organization prevailed. There the civilization was industrial, rather than military. Commerce was accounted a worthy work; not so high as fighting, of course, but still perfectly respectable; and the individual enjoyed a freedom and security unknown elsewhere.

Which type of civilization would endure? That was the great question before the world. Would the soldier and aristocrat, or the merchant and artisan, survive in the struggle which had already begun? The sixteenth century passed, and the contest was decided. The sturdy mechanic had outworn his armoured and tinselled lord. Italy was ruined; Germany broken in two; Spain hopelessly wrecked; France, bled white by civil war, was gasping for breath. But England and Holland stood erect and at ease; and, pausing only to make sure that the victory was theirs indeed, went forth to possess the world. Jamestown and New Amsterdam were the first efforts of the free northern peoples to possess the land they had won.

And not only was Jamestown the first English colony on the continent, but it was the first white settlement that deserved the name of colony at all. The adventures of the Spaniards were not colonizing, but conquest. They were crusaders, going forth to found kingdoms, not settlers seeking out homes. They went to the most densely inhabited parts of the new world, simply because only a dense population of slaves could uphold the costly military type of Spanish civilization. The English came as homemakers. They sought out the unsettled parts of the land, and these they covered with a working civilization. Bad as slavery afterward became in this country, it never had a twentieth part of the influence on our life that the same institution had in Spanish lands. The result is history. The industrial civilization which had beaten militarism on its own ground in the old world, outstripped it with ridiculous ease in the new. Spain had a century's start, yet today two-thirds of the white people on the Western continent speak the English language and live within the borders of the United States.

A Tribute to Virginia

Here is to Virginia, "The Old Dominion" State. At last with the young Confederacy linked her fate. Go search the annals of history back to the days of Abraham; trace Jewish civilization; compare Greek and Roman progress; weigh the crusaders of the middle ages and the reformers of the fifteenth and sixteenth centuries. Then look to the English people who first wrested the great Magna Charta—the Bill of Civil Rights—and human freedom from King John, and implanted these principles first in Virginia with the best blood of England, producing a Washington, a Jefferson, a Patrick Henry, a Madison, a Monroe, a Marshall, a Tyler, a Wise, a Robert E. Lee, a Stonewall Jackson—with thousands as high-toned and patriotic. There she stands superb! With her honour, her chivalry, her patriotism and valour. Her high standard of civilization, unequalled and unexcelled by any people in any age, in any land. In the most trying crisis of any age she bore herself grandly, nobly. As Mother of Presidents and Mother of States. It was her lot to suffer most of all. For four years invaded by hostile armies and burdened by her own defenders, in the great struggles that swayed back and forth. Her homes despoiled, her fields trampled, her sons slain, and her soil drenched in blood. She was steadfast, generous and hospitable to the last. She fed the hungry, clothed the naked, and cared for the sick and bound up the wounded. And not a word of complaint ever came from a Confederate soldier that she ever failed to do what she could for him.

Virginia was all this, notwithstanding she was handicapped by negro slavery, insidiously introduced by Dutch traders. And when it was known that Africans had sense enough to set plants and worm tobacco, New England sagacity and enterprise were quick to supply the demand for slaves and to stock the market until Virginia cried, hold! enough! Negro slavery held her on the low plane of an agricultural state—a producer of cheap raw products. Yet history shows no example of such progress as was made in the civilization of the Negro race. George Washington freed his negroes and turned them loose upon the community. Thomas Jefferson foresaw that a government could not remain half slave and half free. But the steady increase in slave property and its broad extension prohibited its ready abolition. Virginians were not the people to be dictated to by the very people that had pressed slavery upon her. She stood for the right to manage her domestic affairs as she pleased, and was quick to resent outside interference. The clash was inevitable and had to be fought to a finish. North Carolina, her faithful daughter, loves to honour and cherish her Alma Mater. As Virginia, so were all the Southern States—brothers all standing shoulder to shoulder in a common cause.

History of Co. F

This was one of the last companies raised in Cleveland County, and was composed three-fourths of married men. I joined the company as a recruit, 17th of August, 1863, at Halifax, N. C., and was with it constantly in all its service except from the 28th of July, 1864, to the 15th of October, 1864, when I was away at hospital and on sick furlough. It was organized into the Fifty-sixth Regiment at Camp Mangum, near Raleigh, when its captain, H. F. Schenck, was elected major, and B. F. Grigg was elected captain. Captain Grigg was first sergeant, and having served six months with First N. C. Regiment, and having participated in the first battle of the war at Big Bethel, Va., and being a good drill master, naturally succeeded Major Schenck as captain. Lieutenants, Dr. V. J. Palmer, Dick Williams, Alfred Grigg (after Williams was killed); an Irishman by the name of Purse served as third lieutenant for a while. Sergeants, A. J. London, Frank M. Stockton, William London, Pink Shuford, Rufus Gardner, Hezekiah Dedmon. Corporals, T. Jefferson Hord, Thomas J. Dixon, Benjamin A. Jenkins, Lawson A. Bridges, Graham Wilson.

Privates

Those still living June, 1906 marked *

*Allen, Rufus
Blanton, Arthur
Beaver, David
Bedford, James
Cabiness, Thos. P.
Crowder, Joseph
*Carter, W. Jackson
*Cogdall, Perry
Davis, J. Pinkney
Eskridge, Simeon
*Fortenbury, Mark
Gibson, Oliver P.
Glodden, Hosea
*Grigg, Levi
*Hasten, William
Harny, Judson
Kirby, Monroe
Ledford, John
Lutz, Frank
London, Anonymous
Moore, Spencer
Michael, Luther

Nowlin, John H.
Newton
Powell, James S.
Powell, Christopher
*Peeler, James
Philbek, David
Revels, Wesley
Smith, Elijah
Spangler, Johnson
*Teseneer, John A.
Webb, Frank
Weathers, Albert
*Wright, Sanders

Allen, William
*Blanton, Frank
Bookout, Silas
*Blanton, William
*Crowder, Spencer A.
*Crowder, John
Cogdall, Allen
Chitwood, William
Daugherty, Samuel
Eaker, Jesse
*Fortenbury, Anglis
Gaines, Barlet
*Grigg, John
Hoard, Sabert
*Hasten, Frank
Justice, Lewis
Kennedy, Alexander
Louis, Peter
Lucas, Christopher
London, Sidney
Moore, Asbury
Maynard, a South
    Carolinian
Nowlin, Thos. L.
Newton, Little Son
Powell, James
Price, Peter
Phillips, Noah
*Randall, Isaac
Sanders, Griffin
Smith, J. Marcus
*Suttle, D. B. F.
*Wolfe, W. Cathy
Wesson, Dobbins
Wellmon, William
Wright, Winslow

*Beam, Joseph
Barnett, W. Riley
Bookout, Marmaduke
Chitwood, J. Marshall
*Crowder, Mike
Carter, John
*Cogdall, Adney
Davis, Thomas
*Elliott, James C.
Finch, James
*Gantt, Iley
Green, William
Grigg, T. Goode
*Hasten, Samuel
Haynes, Mijamon
Jones, Starlin
Ledford, McKee
*Lutz, Luther
London, Thomas
London, John
*McMurry, Bartlett
*Nowlin, Anderson

Newton, Big Son
Norman, James
*Powell, Isaac
*Peeler, David
Pryor, Pinkney
Richards, Wesley
Sparks, Albert
*Spurlin, Jefferson
Thompson, George
Webb, John
*Weathers, Sidney
White, Moses
Wright, Riley

Making in all 135 men and officers, with probably a few more that died before I joined the company. John H. Nowlin had served three years in a Mississippi regiment before he was transferred to Company F, and he had been wounded twice. O. P. Gibson was transferred to Forty-ninth Regiment, and was severely wounded. Isaac Randall exchanged with Maynard, and went to a South Carolina regiment, and was in the regiment blown up at the Crater. Christopher Powell was transferred from Thirty-eighth Regiment. William Blanton was company commissary. He was elected Lieutenant in Captain David Magness' company, Thirty-eighth Regiment, and transferred. George Thompson was then company commissary. Dobbins Wesson was regiment mail boy, then Rufus W. Gardner took his place. William Green shot and killed himself while hunting deserters. David Philbeck was the first man to die; he died of measles. Ben. A. Jenkins was the last man to die; he died in Point Lookout prison.

The Fifty-sixth Regiment N. C. Troops served under Generals Bob Ransom, Martin Pryor, and then under Brig-Gen. Matt. W. Ransom, with Twenty-fourth, Twenty-fifth, Thirty-fifth and Forty-ninth Regiments N. C. Troops. For more than a year the Fifty-sixth operated on the line from Petersburg, Va., to Wilmington, N. C., in protecting that railroad and coast country. In the spring of 1863, the Fifty-sixth was deployed on picket duty in Gum Swamp, below Kinston; the Federals cut it off and attempted its capture. After some resistance by several companies, they all took to the swamp and escaped, losing a few captured, and field officers losing their horses. Company F was detached, and got away in good order. This little escapade was the source of much merriment with the other regiments, who "poked" much fun at the Fifty-sixth for running at Gum Swamp.

The Fifty-sixth represented all sections of North Carolina, as follows:

Co. A, Captain Hughes, Pasquotank County
Co. B, Captain Roberts, Robeson County

Co. C, Captain White, Currituck County

Co. D, Captain Graham, Orange County

Co. E, Captain Lockhart, Northampton County

Co. F, Captain Grigg, Cleveland County

Co. G, Captain Lanemills, Henderson County

Co. H, Captain Graves, Alexander County

Co. I, Captain Harrell, Rutherford County

Co. K, Captain Alexander, Mecklenburg County

About the 1st of September, 1863, the Fifty-sixth Regiment, except Companys B and E, were detained to assist the Home Guards to arrest deserters and conscripts, and for five months operated in the counties of Randolph, Davidson, Moore, Montgomery, Chatham, Wilkes, Watauga, Ashe and Alleghany. During this time we arrested and sent two thousand men to the front that the militia were unable to manage, killing and wounding thirty-five in making these arrests. During the last two months of this service Company F furnished a provost guard of eighteen men, commanded by Sergeant F. M. Stockton, at regiment headquarters, Ashboro, N. C. About the 20th of January, 1864, the regiment gathered in camp at High Point, N. C., and drilled ten days, and then joined General Pickett's command of six brigades—Hoke's, Ransom's and Clingman's N. C. Brigades, Barton's, Kemper's and Corse's Virginia Brigades. All met at Kinston, N. C., on the 30th of January, 1864, and made an expedition against New Bern, accompanied by a regiment of cavalry, First N. C., under Colonel Dearing, and several batteries of artillery. Set out 31st of January, and struck the enemy at Core Creek on Deep Gully at 3 a. m. on the first day of February, 1864. The Fifty-sixth was with Corse's Brigade. Hoke's Brigade made the attack on the fortified position, supported directly by Corse's Brigade. Some of the forts and block houses were flanked, and the fighting was continuous until

9 a. m., when all positions were taken and the enemy in full flight for New Bern. We got all their camp equipage, five hundred prisoners, four pieces of artillery, commissary and quartermaster supplies, and pursued them ten miles to New Bern, invested the town, and skirmished around for thirty-six hours, then fell back. While on the skirmish line at 1 a. m., 2nd February, we saw a Federal gunboat blown up. Our naval forces had gone down Neuse River in open boats and surprised and captured this vessel, and after taking the prisoners off, blew it up. The enemy were ready to evacuate as soon as we should make the assault, but from some misunderstanding of orders the attack was not made, and General Barton was afterwards court-martialed and acquitted.

We came back to Kinston and hanged twenty-five of those prisoners who were found to be deserters from our army. Then we went to Weldon and put up winter quarters where we had been in camp the summer before. About the 14th of February, a detail was made of twenty-five men from Company F and twenty-five men from Company K, under command of Captain Grigg and Lieutenant Shepherd, to help move the Federal prisoners from Richmond, Va., to Andersonville, Ga. We were on this service until 26th of March. These prisoners were in a pitiable plight and infected with small-pox. William Allen and Pink Pryor caught it from them; don't see why we all did not. During this time or early in March the Brigade made an expedition against Suffolk, Va., and after a running fight with negro cavalry, took that town, but did not hold it long. Capt. Cicero Durham, in command of a skirmish line, drove all before him and charged into the cavalry line and single-handed cut down several men with his own hand. Gilbert Green, of Capt. Jud. Magness' company, was killed in the town, fired upon by some negro troops from a house. The house was fired, and when the negroes jumped out they were shot down. Green was the only man we lost.

On the 14th of April, 1864, we were under light marching orders to leave our knapsacks and carry one blanket. The men were all in fine condition, and of Company F, one hundred answered roll-call and set out on the expedition for Plymouth, N. C., under Gen. R. F. Hoke. The forces consisted of Hoke's and Ransom's N. C. and Kemper's Virginia brigades, First N. C. Cavalry Regiment, and several batteries of field artillery. We went by rail to Tarboro, and on the 15th set out for Plymouth, 65 miles distant, or three days' marching. We arrived at Plymouth Sunday morning, 17th. The cavalry rushed forward and picked up first picket posts, followed by infantry. As they brought prisoners back, we noticed one horse shot in the nose, and a little further on a dead Yankee in the road.

General Hoke sent a truce flag and demanded the surrender of the post. General Wissils, in command, indignantly replied, "Take it." General Hoke replied, "Remove all non-combatants within twenty-four hours."

We threw up earthworks that night. Next day sharp skirmishing took place until the twenty-four hours had expired, then a heavy skirmish line was thrown forward and all the enemy driven inside their defences; then thirty pieces of artillery were brought into position and we began to shell the town. The enemy replied with great spirit, and a terrible duel raged from near sunset until 10 p. m. We were in front of our guns, lying flat, while the shot and shells from both sides hissed, whizzed and bursted over us. While we were engaged with the main fortifications, Hoke's Brigade was taking a detached fort up the river by direct assault.

In addition to the land batteries, the gunboats in the river were hurling huge shells at us. The next day, Tuesday evening, Ransom's Brigade worked its way around east of the town and, after a sharp skirmish fight, drove the Yankee pickets away from a deep creek, where we put in a pontoon bridge and crossed over and took position after dark under a picket and artillery fire. Here we formed for the final attack. The firing soon ceased, as we did not reply, and we lay in line of battle and got a good night's sleep. At first dawn of day we were standing in line in the following order; Twenty-fifth on the right next to the river, Fifty-sixth next, Eighth (from Clingman's Brigade, which was with us in place of Forty-ninth) in centre, then Twenty-fourth and Thirty-fifth on the left, the field officers walking up and down the line quietly talking to the men. "North Carolina expects every man to do his duty. Pay close attention to orders, keep closed up, and press forward all the time. The sooner we can get into the town the better for us."

Hoke's and Kemper's brigades were on the west side. They fired the signal guns, advanced their picket lines as if they were going to assault from that side, while we quietly moved forward and covered half the distance before the fire was opened upon us. Then began the shower of shot and shell. The two regiments on the right soon struck their cattle lot, and we had a drove of cattle in front of us, but coming to a lagoon and swamp we had to let the cattle pass back through our line. Then through water and slush four feet deep we made our way through the swamp and re-formed under cover of a little hill. The three regiments on our left passed around the swamp. We then raised a yell and rushed forward upon the entrenchments and were soon in possession of them, the Yankees falling back and taking shelter behind the buildings, kept up a steady fire upon us as we advanced rapidly. Our field artillery soon came in and opened fire, while the Twenty-fifth swept along the river and captured a fort, and the other regiments drove the balance of the enemy into the big Fort Williamson, on the south side of the fortifications. The Fifty-sixth split into three sections. Maj. John W. Graham advanced the centre faster than the wings and soon planted our flag on the west fortifications. This was a signal for Hoke's and Kemper's brigades to come in from that side. On Monday night of the first attack, at midnight, our ironclad gunboat, *Albemarle*, came down the river and cleared it of all the Yankee shipping, sinking and running off all their gunboats. The *Albemarle* was firing into Fort Williamson. General Hoke demanded the surrender of this fort, but General Wessel was slow in giving answer. When General Hoke began to form his Brigade to assault it, the Stars and Stripes were hauled down and a white flag raised. After three hours of hard fighting, the town with entire garrison, consisting of two fine New York and two Pennsylvania infantry regiments, with cavalry and strong artillery force, and besides the killed and wounded, 2,800 prisoners. The post was strongly fortified and well supplied with military stores and much mercantile goods. As soon as the surrender was made, all our troops were turned loose to help themselves to anything they wished—grocery and dry goods stores richly stocked to select from. Being more than sixty miles from a railroad, and the enemy still close by at Roanoke Island and Washington, we could only supply immediate needs. We were marched out of town that evening.

Nearly all the loss was in Ransom's Brigade, which numbered about six hundred killed and wounded. The Fifty-sixth lost ninety men. Company F—John Webb, shot through the breast; Peter Price, through the lungs; Hosea Gladden, in bowels, and died; Anderson Nolan, Allen Cogdall, Adney Cogdall and William Chitwood were all severely wounded;

Thomas Cabiness and several others wounded. Dr. Lieut. V. J. Palmer was very seriously wounded by having back of thigh cut with piece of shell.

After resting until the 25th of April, we struck out for Washington, N. C. Thirty-five miles march brought us there on the 27th at 10 a. m. The enemy's pickets were driven in and we skirmished around there and were shelled from gunboats until morning of the 29th, when the town was evacuated. Leaving the Sixth Regiment of Hoke's Brigade to garrison it, we moved via Greenville and Snow Hill, crossing Neuse River below Kinston on a pontoon bridge that we carried with us, on to New Bern, crossing Trent River on our pontoon, and going down south side of Trent River, struck the Beaufort railroad, capturing a cavalry picket post of seventy-five men. We laid siege to New Bern and were soon under heavy shelling from the Yankee gunboats. Barton's Virginia Brigade had joined us below Kinston.

After reconnoitring and getting into position twenty-four hours for attack, General Hoke got orders at noon, 7th of May, 1864, to hasten to the relief of Petersburg, Va., that General Butler had landed at City Point with a force of forty thousand, while General Grant was pressing General Lee with overwhelming force through the Wilderness battles. Raising the siege of New Bern, we marched back to Kinston, arriving there the 9th at 8 a. m., where we found trains ready to transport us to Virginia. At 1 p. m. we arrived where Butler's cavalry had cut the railroad between Weldon and Petersburg and were burning bridges and depots and tearing up the road to cut us off. We (Ransom's Brigade) followed close after them all that evening until after midnight, when they left the railroad after tearing up and destroying twenty miles of the road. Here we rested until 8 a. m., May 10th, when trains came out from

Petersburg after us. Boarding the cars with loaded guns, we arrived in Petersburg at 11 a. m. As soon as our train rolled in we could hear the popping of musketry on suburbs, and the greatest excitement prevailed. The citizens, women and children, turned out to greet us. Beautiful ladies showered bouquets of flowers upon us as we marched the streets, with such exclamations as, "We are safe now. These are the brave North Carolinians who have driven the enemy from their own State and have come to defend us. These are the brave boys that took Plymouth," etc. We were marched down the Popular Lawn Hospital grounds to a gushing rock spring, beautiful shade trees and green grass, where we rested until next morning. As soon as we were settled the white ladies and coloured aunties began to pour in upon us with great baskets of everything good to eat and gave us a bountiful feast. Early next morning we moved out and took the Turnpike road towards Richmond, leisurely marching all day while our cavalry were rubbing against the enemy on our right with frequent brisk skirmishes. Out a few miles from Petersburg we passed over the ground where Hagood's Florida Brigade had checked the enemy's advance from that quarter a few days before. The thickets were shattered and remnants of equipments were scattered about, and the bloody places where many had fallen were still visible. Arriving near Drury's Bluff, we lay down to sleep in line of battle beside the Turnpike, facing east. About 2 a. m. the rain falling in our faces woke us, and soon our pickets close by commenced firing. We retained our position until day. Then we moved out on a country road to the right and coming to a turnpike turned into a wheat field at a farm house and formed line of battle in a pouring rain. Two good companies were taken from each of our five regiments and deployed as skirmishers under the command of Capt. Cicero Durham. They did not get

25

out of our sight until they opened fire on the enemy. We then marched a mile east of Turnpike and occupied a good line of earthworks while heavy skirmish fighting was kept up all day. Companys G and I of the Fifty-sixth were on the firing line. Captain Durham made the enemy think we were anxious for a fight. He would charge and drive their skirmishers back on their battle lines and then fall back, and as soon as they advanced, charge and drive them back again, picking up some prisoners every time. Thus it went on all day, while the rain fell in continuous showers.

Next morning, 13th, all was quiet on the lines. In the afternoon we, the Thirty-fifth, Forty-ninth and Fifty-sixth, moved west of Turnpike and, crossing the railroad, occupied some earthworks on a commanding position. The lines ran west then southwest. A nice dwelling stood back of the corner. Generals Hoke and Ransom had dismounted and gone into the house. The Forty-ninth on right, Thirty-fifth centre, Fifty-sixth on left. We were stretched out single file to cover the ground. The enemy was drawing our attention down the railroad towards Petersburg by firing some shells at us, all of which were falling a little short. We were in fine spirits, hoping to see the enemy advance to the open in front, but it had been discovered that the enemy had outflanked us and a force gone around. Captain Durham was deploying his skirmishers in a small field near the house and in our rear. Company H of Fifty-sixth was sent on the skirmish line. Colonel Faison, of Fifty-sixth, was out there, and sent orders to Captain Grigg for eighteen men. I went with them, and we lined up with Company H. Just back of the field was a dense pine thicket. Colonel Faison said: "They don't need you; you Company F men can go back to your company," and he walked back with us. Then the Yankees massed in that pine thicket, ran up to the fence and poured a volley into us. Generals Hoke and Ransom mounted their horses and came over the earthworks through Company F. Ransom, seeing a part of the Fifty-sixth on turn or angle would be exposed to an enfilading or flank fire, said: "Colonel Faison, take your regiment down and form on the railroad." Colonel Faison said, "Major Graham, take those three companies on the left we had about-faced down and form on railroad." Company F went with Major Graham, while Colonel Faison kept the other seven companies there and helped to repulse the Yankees until all could get out. The Twenty-fourth and Twenty-fifth were nearby, and came to the railroad and we formed with them. Captain Durham followed us and was taken off his horse in Company F. One arm was broken and he was shot in the side. His arm was amputated and he died in a few days. Thus ended the career of one of Cleveland County's bravest boys that did battle for that cause. A battalion of picked men was being organized for him to do all the sharp-shooting and skirmishing for the brigade.

Our company, H, had not deployed, and one over half was shot down. We privates all thought had Colonel Faison obeyed Ransom's order to take his regiment out, Thirty-fifth and Forty-ninth would have been captured. As soon as they could stand the Yankees off, they came to the railroad, and we all went up the railroad to the next line of defence, abandoning that line. The Yankees followed us up and fortified a position, and kept up a fire on us all day and night during 14th and 15th. General Ransom was wounded in the arm about 9 a. m. on 15th, standing in rear of Company F, exposing himself, I thought, unnecessarily, in company with some other officer. I was looking at him and expecting it when he was hit. Beauregard had now come up from Charleston and gathered up eighteen or twenty thousand men. Tradition says Jeff Davis told Beauregard to drive Butler away from there; Beauregard said he could not take the responsibility with the force he had.

Jeff Davis told Beauregard to drive Butler away from there. Beauregard said he could not take the responsibility with the force he had.

Jeff Davis: "I will take the responsibility."

Beauregard: "All right, then I'll do the fighting."

On the night of the 14th and 15th of May our Company F was ordered out in the open field in front of our breastworks on picket or vidette duty, and lay all night in the open field under fire from the enemy's sharpshooters.

We did not return the fire, or they would have killed us all. As it was, they could only guess at our position in the dark. The bullets were striking the ground around us with a noise as if they were as large as goose eggs. Mike Crowder was severely wounded while we were taking position.

On Monday morning, 16th of May, a very dark, foggy morning, Hoke's division, I think, with Barton's Virginia Brigade leading the charge, assaulted Butler's right next the river, breaking his strongly fortified line and capturing two thousand prisoners the first dash. Then pressing his broken flank with a strong force and throwing regiment after regiment against his front, carried the entire line by 10 a. m. Ransom's Brigade, commanded by Col. Leroy McAfee, made a front attack west side of Turnpike road, Twenty-fourth, Twenty-fifth and Forty-ninth leading, supported by Thirty-fifth and Fifty-sixth regiments. When our regiment got in the enemy's earthworks their whole line was falling back. James S. Powell and W. Cathey Wolfe, Company F, were wounded. We saw President Davis and General Beauregard together on the field.

Our loss was three thousand killed and wounded. The Turnpike road, over which the wounded were carried, was drenched with blood. The Yankee loss was five thousand killed, wounded and captured. Butler fell back to Bermuda Hundreds, under cover of his gunboats. General Hoke took his old brigade, Clingman's North Carolina, Barton's, Kemper's and Corse's Virginia brigades and hastened to General Lee at Cold Harbor, leaving Ransom's North Carolina, Grace's Alabama, Walker's South Carolina, and Wise's Virginia brigades to look after Butler. These were put in command of Gen. Bushrod Johnson, and remained as Johnson's Division until the close of the war.

Next day we followed Butler and fortified a position close to him and where we were shelled from his gunboats. We extended our picket line to within a few hundred yards of Butler's. On the morning of the 20th of May we got orders to wash our shirts. We had left our knapsacks at Weldon, N. C., on the 14th of April, and had had four weeks of strenuous campaign in North Carolina and two weeks in Virginia. Six weeks without a chance to wash or change our shirts, and now we had no vessels to warm water, so the only chance was to wash in a small creek. Our shirts from sweat and grime had gotten so dirty and stiff they would almost stand upright. Shirts were washed and hung on bushes to dry, but before all got dry, or at 1 p. m., we were ordered to fall into line for another battle. We wanted Butler's picket line for our line to crowd him closer and fortify our picket line. Both picket lines had rifle pits and were hard to take at best. The Thirty-fifth and Fifty-sixth were ordered to take the picket line in front of our brigade. The Thirty-fifth deployed and charged forward, followed by Fifty-sixth in line of battle. The Thirty-fifth was driven back, and Fifty-sixth charged up and found a strong line of battle in the rifle pits. When we got in forty or fifty yards of them we were ordered to fire, lay down, load, shoot. When we had fired five rounds under a terrible hail of bullets at so close range, some one said, "They are flanking us." Then the order to retreat. We were in an old pine field with some undergrowth of oak bushes, while the Yankee line was on the edge of a dense wood. We fell back and rallied when some regiments of Walker's South Carolina Brigade came in on our right and with a yell charged on the Yankees, who were advancing on us. The Twenty-sixth lined up with them and helped to drive the Yankees back to their line of rifle pits. Our line lay down and kept up our fire on them until our ammunition was pretty well spent. The Fifty-sixth had ninety-six killed and wounded. Company F lost four killed and nine severely wounded and several slightly wounded. Our killed were left where they fell and were buried by the enemy. They were Second Lieutenant Dick Williams, a brave soldier and a man loved by all his company; privates Thomas P. Cabaniss, Christopher Powell and Winslow Wright, all good soldiers. Powell and Cabaniss were single men. Cabaniss was killed by my side, and my left cheek was blistered by a hot bullet. Frank Webb and J. M. Smith died of their wounds. Jefferson Spurlin lost a leg and Johnson Spangler lost an arm. Sam. Daugherty, Peter Louis, Morman Bookout, B. McMurry and Monroe Kirby were all severely wounded. That night we fortified our picket line, and General Walker reconnoitring his position was wounded and captured. We were so close to them that firing was kept up all night and for several days following. On the evening of the 22d a truce was had to bury some dead between the lines. And the graves of our dead were visited. A few days after this a skirmish line from our brigade charged and took this Yankee skirmish line which had cost us so much on the 20th of May. Here we lay in the burnt woods, within a few hundred yards of the enemy, firing and shelling every day until the 1st of June. Our brigade crossed James River on a pontoon bridge and passed through the Seven Pines battle ground to the Chickahominy River, where we spent a few days in sight of the enemy's position on the north side, the picket of each making the river the line. We then came up to Chafin's farm or bluff and spent about a week, until the night of 15th of June. We marched all night to Petersburg, Va.

Grant had now advanced the head of his column, and our little force of four brigades must hold him in check until Lee could come. So we had to vacate our lines between the Appomattox and James rivers and throw our main forces in defence of Petersburg, where we arrived at sunrise. The Fifty-sixth was sent up the north side of the Appomattox to guard the cotton factories from a cavalry raid, while the other four regiments went to the front and were fighting all day. During the day Butler's forces destroyed the railroad between Petersburg and Drury's Bluff. After dark we joined the brigade on the Turnpike and started back toward Drury's Bluff. We only went a few miles, feeling for the Yankees, but were kept on foot nearly all night. Next morning, 17th, some flat cars came after us and landed us in Petersburg, and we hurried to the front. Grant had taken some of the outside lines, and we formed a line in a corn field and threw up breastworks under shelling and picket fire. While fortifying our line, Joseph Crowder was killed and James Bedford and Simon Eskridge were mortally wounded. About 2 p. m. Grant began to assault our line next to the river on our left, and kept it up for a long time. Our boys would yell when they would drive them back and pass the word along the line, "Repulsed with great loss; hold your position at all hazards; Lee's army will be here at 10 tonight." Near sunset they took the position held by Wise's Brigade. We were under moving orders at once, and a little after dark the Thirty-fifth and Fifty-sixth, and probably some of our other regiments, joined Grace's Alabama Brigade to retake the lost ground. The full moon was an hour or two high. After a quick but desperate struggle the line was retaken, to be abandoned next morning. All our historians give the Alabamians all the credit and none mention the North Carolinians. In the night and through the woods I thought at the time all our brigade was there. I know the Thirty-fifth was next to us and sustained heavy loss. About 2 a. m. we fell back to a new and last position in front of Cemetery Hill, now known as the Crater, leaving a strong skirmish line with orders to hold as long as they could and to fall back as slowly as possible. This was to enable us to fortify another line which had only been staked off the day before.

At daybreak on the 18th we were standing in single file, half line of battle, when we heard Grant's massive columns charge on our skirmishers and take the last ditch between them and Petersburg. Our artillery was all in position on our last line. Lee's army had not come, and Grant only had a half line of tired and worn-out soldiers in his front, standing in open field between him and Petersburg. The Fifty-sixth in the night battle was on the left flank, and did not suffer like the other regiments. Of Company F, Noah Phillips, was killed, Spencer Moore and Wesley Revels captured.

When the enemy got those earthworks, we expected them on us at once. Having only seven or eight tools to the company, we fell to work with our bayonets to make a hole to squat in. We had bluffed them so the night before that they thought Lee had arrived, and waited several hours before they drove in our brave skirmishers that held them in a wood until we had a good ditch. Though we had had but little sleep and rest for three days and nights, we moved dirt in a hurry. We occupied a most commanding position. Fifty-sixth covered the ground now known as the Crater.

Some branches, broad fields, with some skirts of woods lay in front of us. About 10 a. m. our skirmishers were driven in after an heroic resistance. Then the long blue lines came gleaming on. The officers galloping over the field, while battery after battery were taking position under the fire of our artillery and opening fire on us. Then to our left, winding down a ravine, we saw Longstreet's column coming in, and soon came crowding up our ditch Anderson's Division, South Carolinians and Georgians. Most of these regiments were very short, and I was eager to note what these battle-scarred veterans who had just been fighting for a month through the Wilderness thought of the situation. Tired from an all-night's march, but as soon as they got in position they stripped blankets and piling handfuls of cartridges on the breastworks got up on the parapet, took a look in front and said, "This is a good place; we would like for them to come on ten lines deep, so we won't waste any lead."

Then they quietly sat down. We were now too much crowded, and our regiment was ordered out and I was ordered to help carry some boxes of ammunition that belonged to our company. The Fifty-sixth started back in a run across a broad field under heavy fire. Longstreet's men objected to our taking the ammunition, and while we were parleying about it, Captain Gee, of Ransom's staff, came along and I called his attention to it, and he said, "Oh, leave it here, those men may need it." We were now left and started around to go up the ravine and came up with Lieutenant Davis, of Company G, Fifty-sixth, who said: "Fifty-sixth is just ordered back to rest. A part of the companies on the right of the battery (at Crater) are still here. The Yankees had opened such a heavy fire they would not try to get out. There is going to be an interesting time here, and I want to see it out. If you will stay with me I will take care of you." Six or seven of his company were with him. Soon Sergt. Wm. London and Isaac Randall of Company F joined us. Peter Price, who had been shot through the lung at Plymouth, was wounded in the thigh as they fell back, and Mayor Graham was wounded in the arm. We were now about one hundred and fifty yards to the left of the Crater battery. At about 1 p. m. three lines of battle made a desperate effort to break our lines on the right. We could see them form an advance like they were on dress parade, raise their cheer and rush close to our line; then our volleys would knock them into confusion. In the meantime they were bringing line after line down to the branch in our front, where they could find cover under the hill. We would let them get about midway in a field, then we could get about two rounds into them before they got under cover. Soon they began to charge us from this close quarter, but two or three rounds would drive them back under cover shelter. Finally they crawled up the side of a hill and massed seven flags within two hundred yards of us, and lay there until night. The heavy firing of musketry and artillery lasted until midnight before we could get out. Captain Roberts, of Company B, Fifty-sixth, had his head shot off. One tall, dark-eyed South Carolinian was shot in the head and killed by my side. He was a brave man, taking deliberate aim every shot. One other man was wounded close to me.

A. P. Hill's corps got to Petersburg at night of 18th. Next morning Jesse Lattimore, of Company F, Thirty-fourth N. C. Regiment, visited us, and was still in good spirits of whipping the Yankees. We told him they hadn't brought men enough with them and their regiments were too small. After resting twenty-four hours we moved right and worked on some fortifications.

On the evening of 24th of June, Wilcox's Division attacked Grant's left, supported by our brigade and a part of

Johnson's division. It was called the battle of Huckleberry Swamp. The enemy was strongly entrenched, and we fell back after dark. We were only slightly under fire. We recalled that Lafayette Beam, of Capt. David Magness' company, Thirty-eighth Regiment, was killed that evening. We occupied Scales Brigade camp, and about midnight they came in on us and we all lay and slept until late next morning.

The next night we took position on the branch to the left of the Crater. We had always felt pretty safe in the earthworks until here Grant began to shell us with mortars, throwing huge shells up to fall on us or to burst over us and the fragments rain upon us; so now began the most serious time when we could not get rest day nor night except under incessant fire. The left of our brigade rested on the Norfolk railroad, and we held this position in the open fields under a July sun for six weeks, the regiments changing position every week. Our food was miserable—musty meal and rancid Nassau bacon. Our bread was cooked at the wagon yard on canal, west side of Petersburg. When the bread had been cooked twelve hours it would pull out like spider-webs. We were on picket or fatigue duty nearly every night. One-third had to stand to arms all the time, and from 2:30 a. m. all had to stand to arms until sunrise. The two lines were on an average five hundred yards apart.

On the 11th of July, while working on a covered way to the rear, I was wounded in the left arm above the elbow, the ball grazing and bruising the inside of the arm. I was disabled and sent back to field hospital for a few days, during which time I caught measles. Then after a week in the trenches I was sent back to the hospital at Richmond. The men were now breaking down faster under the awful strain and bad fare; many were taking typhoid fever, and nearly all had dysentery. A train load of sick and wounded were being shipped to Richmond every day.

I left on the 28th of July. It was known that the Yankees were undermining our works, and we were tunnelling all around to meet them, but our tunnel at the Crater missed them about fifty feet. On the 30th the Crater was exploded under Elliott's South Carolina Brigade, formerly Walker's, on our right. I shall not attempt a description of that memorable event farther than to say Ransom's Brigade, commanded by Colonel Rutledge of Twenty-fifth, held its position and helped to retake the lost ground, though none of our historians seem to be advised of that fact. Up to this time, Lieutenant Grigg, Perry Ross, Arthur Blanton and Alexander Kennedy had been wounded, and soon after Starlin Jones was mortally wounded. When I convalesced I found John Carter and Dobbins Wesson in the same ward with typhoid fever, and I went to see them every day. One evening when I called, Carter said he was glad to see me, that he wanted to talk with me, for he was going to die. I tried to encourage him, but he said he could not live long. He said he was not afraid to die, that he had always tried to live right, and that it was a great consolation that he had never done anything that would reflect on his people left behind. Thus, before the rising of another sun, a good and true man passed to his reward. A few days after when I visited Wesson he told me that he was in great trouble, that his wife had quit writing to him, etc. I tried to encourage him, when the ward master beckoned to me and said, "You need not pay any attention to him. He is delirious and don't know what he is talking about. He jumped out of the window and we had to catch him and bring him back. If you know his people you can write them that he will not live until tomorrow morning."

I wrote them to that effect. He was a brave and faithful soldier and loved by his comrades.

Of the twenty-five of Company F that died that summer

of sickness, I will mention four of my mess, who were all good and true soldiers and participated in all the battles up to squat. Thomas Davis, Riley Barnett, John Ledford and Thomas L. Nowlin. While I was away, Ransom's Brigade was in the battle of Ream's Station on Weldon railroad, in August, and Louis Justice and Migamon Haynes were killed. Sergt. F. M. Stockton, Luther Lutz and William Chitwood, and probably others, were wounded.

I got back to the company the 15th of October, after a sixty-days furlough, and found our brigade resting left of Appomattox River. Here we remained through the long, hard winter, under fire day and night. During this time Lieutenant Purse was wounded, also Wesley Richards and Sergeant William London mortally wounded. I can not see how we escaped so well, but we learned to lay low, dig holes and contrive bomb-proofs. Then Spencer Crowder used to say that we had Uncle Johnnie London to pray for us. Spencer tried to quit swearing, and we thought he had succeeded, but the last battle we were in he cursed the Yankees as bad as ever. We fortified our position and had portholes for our sharpshooters made of sand bangs and iron plates. Besides the hard fare, we suffered for want of fuel. Our company only got eight or ten sticks of green pine wood per day most of the time. During the winter we got coffee and some canned beef, which helped us greatly. Governor Vance tried to give us a Christmas dinner, but it was only a quart of little Irish potatoes. Our wages were raised from $11 to $15 per month, but they quit paying us at all and owed us for three or four months at the close. The following prices prevailed: Bacon, $10 lb.; pork and beef, $5 lb.; peas, $1 qt.; corn meal, $1.25 qt.; rice, $1 lb.; salt, $1; sweet potatoes, medium, $1 each, and everything else in proportion.

On the 15th of January, 1865, I was detailed to report to

General Ransom's headquarters for special duty, and met a force of several others from brigade. We were taken in command by Lieut. A. Clate Sharp, of Forty-ninth, to boat wood down the river and canal for the men in the trenches. We were soon comfortably quartered at our wagon yard. Here we went seven miles up the canal and two miles up the river into another canal, where we got the wood. This was a real picnic all the time. With three men to the boat, we would bring down four cords of wood on a boat. While out there I would often see General Lee, nearly always by himself, riding around leisurely. I got rations from home and fared sumptuously, while the poor fellows in the ditches were having it rough. They were now trimmed out to one man to the yard. About the first of March about a dozen of Company F concluded they had enough of it, and all started for home, taking their guns with them. They had gotten information from me that there were no guards next to the river, and succeeded in getting through. I will not name them here. They nearly all had been good and faithful soldiers who had borne more hardships than I. They had been in those bleak and bloody trenches for nearly nine months. The annual spring campaign was coming on, and every private knew that resistance could not much longer be sustained. On the 15th of March my detail ended, and we were relieved from the ditches and went to Hotches Run, ten miles away.

Grant was pressing Lee's right, and about 3 a. m. on March 25th, Lee attacked Grant in front of our old position next to the river and carried it with little or no loss. We went in to hold it, and after day they attacked us with a heavy force, and holding the lines on both our flanks, after two hours of hard fighting, turned our right flank and compelled our right to fall back or surrender. The enemy held a fort close on our left, and when they came swarming over the hill on our right and pressing our front we had to surrender with two thousand on that end of the line. All of Company F that were together, thirty-four in all, including Captain and Lieutenant Grigg, Lieutenant Dr. V. J. Palmer, had been in front of our line, and seeing the predicament, slipped out and escaped without coming back through the company. George Thompson was mortally wounded. This was the last of Company F, except five or six rallied by Lieutenant Palmer. The spring before we started out with one hundred, this spring we had forty men in line.

We took our position an hour or two before day. The Yankees had three strong lines of earthworks, with stockade in front, but they only had a skirmish line holding it, while their comfortable encampments were in the rear. We could easily have taken the lines on our left to Appomattox River when we first went in, but it was soon strongly reinforced. As we were marched back to the rear we met battery after battery of field artillery coming in. An artilleryman said, "Johnnies, if you had held them works an hour longer we would have had five hundred guns and cannons playing on you."

We were soon back in our camps and marched around through them for three miles to General Meade's headquarters. In some camps the men were playing ball and frolicking like no enemy was near. Others were falling into line of march; others had muskets stacked ready to fall in at a moment's notice. Far back in the rear endless columns were marching to the left flank of their lines to outflank Lee's right. At Meade's headquarters we were joined by two thousand more of our men who had been captured that morning on Hotche's Run. About 2 p. m. we were reviewed by General Grant and President Lincoln, riding horseback, followed by a troop of cavalry and a number of fine carriages containing officers and ladies. They marched by us and returned and came back by us, where we were in the open along the road. We were then put on some flat or freight cars and shipped to City Point. There we were put inside their large barrack enclosure where their own men were kept under the same guard with us. The next morning they gave us some boiled fat pork and a handful of hardtack. As we came down we passed through Sheridan's cavalry camp of thirty thousand strong.

On Sunday evening, March 26th, General McHenry, a white-headed old man, commanding the post, got upon a barrel and made a speech. He said the war would soon be over, and that President Lincoln had offered amnesty to all who would lay down their arms or desert the Confederate army and come over to the Union side, and that they would be allowed to go North and work. He said that no doubt some of us had wished to desert and quit fighting and had not had a chance to do so, and now he would give us a chance to take the oath of allegiance to the United States if we would volunteer to do so. He would send such up to Washington and see if President Lincoln would accept it and allow them to take the oath and go North and be free from war. When the call for deserter volunteers was arranged, the greatest fun started among the four thousand prisoners. They would make all kinds of humorous remarks about the deserter volunteers. When one would step out, "You are welcome to him; he is as cowardly as any of your hirelings. There goes another; we are glad to get rid of him, for he never was any good," etc. About thirty volunteered and were removed from their fellows. Then he called for three hundred volunteers who wished to be exchanged at once—sent up to Richmond, where they could go to fighting again. We raised a yell, and about two hundred rushed forward. He then called, "Come on, all who want more fighting." There was much stir, comrades hunting up each other so as to keep together. Company F rallied and joined the fighting column, except five or six, who held back and afterwards went up to Washington with the deserter volunteers. We were marched to the wharf and put on a steamboat that carried us to Point Lookout Prison, Maryland, instead of Richmond for exchange. At the time we volunteered so briskly we did not believe we would be exchanged, and its very evident that not many wished to be, for they all believed that the war would be over in a few weeks.

While on the wharf a nice, clever old citizen came up to me, a beardless boy, and entered into a conversation. He said, "It is very fortunate for you that you were taken prisoner. You are in the hands of a civilized and Christian people who will treat you well and you will not have to fight any more. The war will be over in six months, and you can then return to your loved ones at home." I heard him patiently, and he felt he was making a good impression on me. Then I retorted: "You are putting it off for six months now, are you? I thought you said you would whip us in three months at the start." He turned away and seemed to lose interest in me. I was from the inside and could have told him the war would be over in six weeks.

We had a good voyage. Stopped a half hour at Fortress Monroe, where there was a great deal of shipping, including war vessels of all nations. We arrived at Point Lookout, Md., at sunset. Our names were recorded and we were overhauled and ushered into prison. There were about three thousand there when we arrived, on the first boat load of the spring campaign. We were assigned quarters in tents already occupied. I thought they would be glad to see us and hear from home, but they seemed mad and asked very few questions that night. But we soon learned that talking was not allowed after dark, as white guards walked the streets inside, while negro sentinels were on the outside parapet. We were always interested in the newcomers, who continued to come for two or three weeks, until the number was increased to twenty-three thousand. Point Lookout lays between Chesapeake Bay and Potomac River, and is nearly surrounded by water. The prison on the Chesapeake side was drained into that bay, and was an ideal place for a military prison, and was considered one of the most healthful prisons. It was enclosed by a high plank fence with two gates, opening to bay and one for entrance on southeast corner. It was divided into ten or twelve divisions, with nearly as many cook-houses, one chapel and school-house, eight wells, no two of which contains the same kind of water. The water was strong *coperas*, *alum*, and some nearly fair freestone. The Confederate government had an agent there, a Methodist preacher by the name of Morgan and a South Carolinian. His business was to look after the welfare of the prisoners, to distribute clothing, etc., very little of which was distributed after we got there. He ran the schools and regulated religious worship in the chapel. We got for a day's ration three-quarters of a pound of loaf bread and six crackers, one pint of soup with a spoonful or two of beans and potatoes in it. About one-quarter pound of fat boiled pork two days, one-half pound fresh beef or mutton one day, and one-half pound of fish (mackerel or codfish) four days in each week. We had no fuel and had to eat fish raw. We got plenty of soap, but nothing to warm water with to wash. We had access to the bay for washing and bathing. There were several details to work on outside of prison, for which we got tobacco and some extra rations. When outside about the wharves we could get a little wood, such as barrel staves, chips and pieces of planks. There were two or three hundred men taken out every fair day to work, and I got out a good deal, was on a regular detail for two or three weeks, which was a great help. The hospital grounds adjoined the prison, and many were in the hospital. It was reported that the death rate some days was more than twenty. Only one of our company died there—Benjamin Jenkins.

Lee's surrender was celebrated by firing signal guns for twenty-four hours. Then Lincoln's death was honoured by all flags half-mast and firing one-half-hour guns for twenty-four hours.

Those fellows who volunteered to take the oath and were sent to Washington had been refused by President Lincoln, but they were all discharged first. Major A. G. Brady was in command of the post. We got no mail or papers. There was a bulletin board for posting orders and news.

There were negroes who had been captured in the Confederate army that remained true and preferred staying with us instead of taking the oath and going free. Also a large number of English sailors, blockade runners, West India negroes, and political prisoners all together. When they began to discharge us about the 6th of June, thirty-two were called out at a time and stood under the Stars and Stripes and took the oath of allegiance together and subscribed to the same in the record books. I got out the 12th of June, and was landed in Richmond on the night of the 13th. Here we were bountifully supplied with rations and given railroad transportation. Everything had now changed. Richmond and all the principal towns were swarming with Federal troops. We remained in Richmond two days on account of a washout, and did not reach home until the 20th of June.

I will state that Lieut. V. J. Palmer and the four or five men with him were captured at Five Forks when the lines were broken. About the first of April, Lieutenant Palmer had his men to load for him, and he stood on the parapet and fired as fast as the guns could be handed to him, until he was surrounded. In the last battle, on the 25th March, 1865, Lieutenant Palmer, with several others, took a position in front of the lines in some narrow drain ditches, where they could keep up a continual fire, while the main line only fired when the enemy advanced in force. During this time T. J. Dixon shot down a brave Yankee at close range, and said, "Boys, don't shoot him any more." L. A. Bridges brought down several of the bravest Yankees at close range. The Yankee who took Bridges' gun said, "You have been using it; it is pretty hot." Bridges said, "Yes, I got it from you and have made the best use of it I could. You can have it; I reckon it belongs to you."

Among those who were never seriously wounded or sick, but were always in their places, were First Sergt. Andy London, who stood at the head of Company F in every battle; Sergt. H. Dedmon, Spencer A. Crowder, Jno. A. Tesseneer, Flay Gantt, Samuel Hasten, Graham Wilson, T. J. Hoard, Sabert Hoard, Joseph Beam, David Peeler and L. A. Bridges. Lieut. V. J. Palmer and Alfred Grigg were always at their posts except while disabled by wounds. Peter Price died last July, James Finch died last year, Lieut. Alfred Grigg moved to Kentucky, Jno. Grigg to Louisiana, Frank Hasten to Tennessee.

Supplemental to History of Company F

The names of Joseph Hasten and Ephraim Wilson, who died early in the service, and Jesse Willis, a senior recruit who served faithfully to the end, were omitted. These are all I can get up. My comrades at this time can give me but little information. People ask how I can recollect so well after so many years. I kept a diary of all important events. Then my mother, who is still living, has all the letters I wrote home during my service in the army. I had nine first cousins in the regular army, and only two survived the war, and they were both severely wounded twice, and I am the only survivor, though I have an uncle living, my mother's brother, Dr. Thos. L. Carson, who was at General Lee's surrender.

Confederate Monument
at Shelby

The Soldier's Monument at Shelby seems to be all that could be desired from anyone's standpoint. There's nothing boastful, nothing flattering or inconsistent. It simply expresses a patriotic duty performed in the greatest crisis in the history of our country. That generation passed through an ordeal second to none in the annals of modern history. Their descendants by whom it is erected have no apologies to make. The massive granite column, to last for ages, will tell the simple story of pride in the heroic fortitude of such ancestry—and will ever be an inspiration to the rising manhood of coming generations. It is most fitting that it is erected now after more than forty years of candid deliberation. If it had been erected thirty years ago it would only have represented our fallen heroes. Ten years ago, when it was first suggested to rear a monument for all Confederate soldiers, living and deceased, the living generally protested, thinking it egotistical or boastful to erect a monument to themselves. But the daughters were too enthusiastic to wait for all the old soldiers to die, and now all old soldiers approve their course and are most grateful for the monument to their comrades, which by and by will stand for all.

The statue on the monument is a good specimen of the stalwart private soldier, and would well represent Private Charles Blanton, of the Fifty-fifth N. C. Regiment, who once captured fourteen prisoners on the skirmish line. Having heard his comrades tell of this heroic deed a few years ago, I asked Mr. Blanton how he did it. He said: "We were ordered to drive the Yankee skirmishers back and locate their battle line. As we advanced on them we saw several taking shelter in a rifle pit, when six or eight of us made a rush to take the pit, and when I got there they ducked down and looked scared, and I ordered them to thrown down their guns and get out of there quick, and they obeyed promptly. As I stepped behind them I saw that I was alone—the others having all been shot down—and seeing their battle line laying flat close by, ordered my prisoners to double-quick to the rear, and I trotted them out all right. When I commanded them to surrender, I thought my comrades were close by, and I had them under good control before I knew any better."

Mrs. Stonewall Jackson refusing a $1,200 pension, while indigent widows and veterans only get a pittance, may cause them to get $150,000 more than heretofore. It is the happiest thought that our countrymen still appreciate most highly the principle that money can not buy. Mrs. Jackson belongs to history, linked to a name that will live through the ages, an inspiration to the highest ideals of patriotic devotion, that bring most desirable achievements that untold generations will be proud to honour.

A Patriotic Recruit

The soldiers life, even in the most strenuous and dangerous campaigns, finds some relief in jest and laughter, like
flowers strewn along the thorny paths of hardships. When
you hear an old soldier boast of his exploits and miraculous
escapes, you can credit him for having been both a good
forager and a good dodger. The best soldiers are ambitious,
patriotic, jovial, patient and uncomplaining.

When our Company F, Fifty-sixth Regiment, had been
in the Camp of Instruction a few weeks, a young, enthusiastic recruit came in. He showed all the marks of a good
soldier, even to a very fine opinion of himself. He was eager
to take a stand in the front rank from the start; and he was
speedily supplied with the regulation equipment. Then he
called on some of the boys at a game of marbles, who interrogated him about his outfit, and inquired if he had got
his marbles.

He: "Do I get marbles?"

They: "Of course every soldier is allowed a set of marbles."

He: "And where do I get my marbles?"

"You will find your marbles at the Colonel's tent, but
when you go after them you must salute the Colonel."

He: "Salute how?"

"This way: Catch your hat with this hand, raise the other
hand, fingers extended, and strike out this way."

After practicing him for awhile, they told him that would

do—he had it right. Then he bolted for the Colonel's tent with all the assurance with which he would accost a township constable. The Colonel was a West Pointer and as dignified and austere as the Czar of all the Russias. After saluting the Colonel, he said, "Colonel, I have just come in and drawed my outfit and have called in to get my marbles."

The Colonel: "The h—ll you say! Report to your quarters at once or I'll have you put in the guard-house."

When he came back, he looked like a bucket of cold water had been thrown on his patriotic enthusiasm. They inquired, "Did you get your marbles?"

He: "No!"

"What did the Colonel say?"

"He cussed me and threatened to put me in the guardhouse."

The reader can imagine what a laugh they had at the breaking in of a real good soldier, who proved faithful to the end. But ever afterwards, whenever he got on a "high hoss," some one would ask him what the Colonel said when he went after his marbles.

A Bad Case of Itch

In the fall of 1863, while my regiment, the Fifty-sixth North Carolina, was on detail service arresting conscripts and deserters in the middle and western counties, our company headquarters then being at Hannah's Cross Roads in Davidson County, a stout, strapping boy of 18 came from Catawba County to join the army with us. He had two uncles in our company who were off with a detachment; and he, being a stranger to all present, and noticing that he had a bad case of itch, all stood aloof from him. After he had been in camp a few days Iley Gantt got a short furlough to visit his sick wife. He, noticing Gantt's arrangements for going home, inquired what he was going home for. Ike Powell said, "We are sending Gantt home because he has got the each."

He: "Well, I've got the each."

P.: "Yes, I see you have, and what did you come here with the each for. We've got trouble enough here without the each."

He: "Well, if you say so I'll go home too, for I am getting mighty tired of this place anyhow."

P.: "Well, that would be the best thing you could do."

He: "But I've eat up all the rations I brought from home, and I haint got nothing cooked to eat, and I can't cook—never cooked any in my life."

P.: "Then I'll tell you what you do; you go to Capt. Grigg

and tell him you want a man detailed to cook some rations to do you home; tell him you are going with Gantt, and that you will stay away from here until you are plumb well of the each."

The young recruit bolted to the Captain, who soon set him straight on army rules and regulations.

Longstreet's Corps Was
On the Way to Chickamauga

The same fall I was at High Point, N. C., and saw Longstreet's Corps pass. The trains all stopped there and I mingled and talked much with them. I never saw soldiers in higher spirits. As they had come through Raleigh, they had destroyed the late ex-Governor W. W. Holden's *Raleigh Standard* printing press.

They exhibited papers fastened to sticks like flags, with handfuls of type. Holden had been advocating peace and they considered him a traitor to the South. They said those western Yankees had been having things their own way out there, but Lee's men were going to give them something that they would not forget soon. "We will put them in a trot like we have been chasing them out of Virginia." They were travelling on freight and flat-cars, with as many on top of freight boxes as inside.

About a week after that we were at High Point again, conveying some arrested conscripts to Raleigh, when train load after train load of Federal prisoners passed going from Chickamauga to Richmond. The trains stopped and we talked with those western prisoners and found them very sassy and determined about the Union.

One big, red-whiskered fellow said to me: "What you fellers doing back here so far in the rear?"

We replied: "We have plenty of men at the front to attend to you fellows. We are just resting and having a good time."

He replied, "Yes, d—n you; I guess you are back here hunting for conscripts and trying to force good Union men into your d—d army."

His train pulled out and we let him go at that, but thinking from the grit he displayed that he must be a Tennessean or Kentuckian.

Shooting an Outlaw

While operating in Randolph County, N. C., in September, 1864, we wounded in the foot and captured a man who had not been in the army but was said to head a band of outlaws. His name was Northcut. He was tried by a little drumhead court marshal and shot on short notice one mile north of Ashboro as we were leaving that section for Wilkes County, where there was a strong Union sentiment hard to hold down. After operating in the mountains several months, where much apple brandy, fat beef, milk and honey abounded, we returned to Randolph and the adjoining counties of Davidson, Moore, Montgomery and Chatham, where there was much work to do. Here we began pressing property, especially horses and feed, from the disloyal to force them to bring in their conscript sons, and soon a number of our company was mounted, only intending to use the horses while operating in that vicinity; but Governor Vance, being advised of it, complained to the Confederate War Department and threatened to turn his militia loose on us and drive us from the State if such conduct was not stopped and all property pressed promptly turned over to the original owners—and we had to come down off our high horses and take it afoot again. Up to that time I had not developed quite courage enough to steal a horse, but was caught red-handed with a good mount in this temporary "critter company."—a furloughed man having given me his horse. So my dignity was shocked when I had to come down from my self-promoted position to a flatfooted infantryman again.

Removing Federal Prisoners from Richmond, Va., to Andersonville, Ga.

February and March, 1864

I was on a detail and made three trips *via* Raleigh, Charlotte, Columbia to Branchville, S. C. These prisoners had been confined on Belle's Island, in James River, and were in a most pitiable condition—half starved, half naked. Most of them had been in prison for months and very few had a change of garments. They were ragged, lousy, filthy and infested with smallpox, and most of them had diarrhoea and scurvy and were so weak that when they would swing down out of box-cars their legs would give away when their feet struck the ground, and they would fall in a heap on the ground. I don't think they got anything to eat except a little bread and meat, mostly cornbread. They were transferred in box-cars, forty packed into a car. We sometimes stopped at Raleigh to change cars, and always stopped at Charlotte twelve to twenty-four hours. We ran up the Seaboard to where it crossed the Statesville Railroad, then in the woods. A small branch ran under both roads east and north of crossing, with embankments on south and west, and we put them out there, where they had free access to the branch. One night several crawled up a drain ditch from branch along railroad and got out between the guard; others were caught in the act and stopped.

Old man Tyree, of Company K detail, whose home was not far away, said he could get some bloodhounds that would run them down. He was sent after the dogs and they were put on their tracks after they had been gone four or five hours, and followed them about thirty miles and caught them. The next time we stopped there, at 2 a. m., they, the prisoners, seemed restless, a number being up and moving around near the guard lines. Two or three made a break through the guard lines and escaped in the darkness. Several shots were fired at them, which awoke and roused up the whole camp. They were ordered to lay down, but would not obey, even when the officers ordered us to fire into them. But instead of firing into them, as we were ordered, tried firing a few shots over them, which had the effect to make them lay down. The officers then went among them and told them if anyone got up before day he would be shot down. But still, occasionally, one would get up and a guard would fire over him. At last one of the guards shot and killed one. That might have been omitted, though we had orders to do so. All the guards deplored that rash action. An old, sick Irishman fell in the branch and died that night. I noticed after the war six or eight graves at that wayside camp. Those who escaped that night probably got through, as we never heard of them again.

While on guard in the car with them some of them twitted us about being afraid of our officers. I told them our officers were kind and treated us well; that I had been in the army seven months and had never seen a man bucked and gagged; and, turning to a serious-looking Irishman, who was listening with interest, but had said nothing, I asked him if he had ever seen anything of that kind in their army.

He answered, "Yes, my friend; I've been bucked and gagged meself many a time."

That was a clincher for me that ended the discussion. The bad treatment of prisoners on both sides makes one of the darkest pictures of that war. We understand statistics show the mortality to be 13 per cent on the Federal side to 9 per cent on the Confederate. My own experience in a Federal prison at the close of the war, while very disagreeable, was much better than those poor fellows were getting with us. But when we take into consideration the superior resources of the United States, they were, to say the least, equally negligent and resentful to their helpless enemies. Point Lookout Federal prison will be treated on in another chapter.

Navigating the Appomattox River

It has been mentioned in a former chapter that I was on a detail in winter, commencing the 15th day of January, 1865, to boat wood for the men in the trenches. The detail for Ransom's brigade, composed of six men from each of the five regiments, commanded by Lieut. A. C. Sharpe, of Forty-ninth Regiment. Those from my regiment, Fifty-sixth North Carolina, were Company B, ... McMillan; Company D, ... Parker; Company F, J. C. Elliott (this writer); Company G, Wm. A. Condrey; Company I, Thomas Robbins; Company K, Calvin Deweese.

We went back to the canal, which ran seven miles up the river, then two miles in the river up into another two-mile canal, and then into the river again. One mile above the basin or boat landing at Petersburg there were several locks through which boats were raised and lowered, and just below the locks there was a small creek, which ran through a stone culvert under the canal. General Lee had built a high dirt dam across that creek and backed the water on the Yankees and drowned out a part of their lines and forced them back. Besides, this big pond protected our position in that quarter. While we were waiting a few days to get our boats ready, this big dam broke loose and the water came in a solid wall about forty feet high, and striking the canal culvert swept it away, and also cleaned out the south side railroad bridge just below. Then the canal had to cross this creek on a wooden trestle, and while it was being built we had to haul wood at night on railroad from towards Richmond. The enemy had a battery on the Chesterfield side that shelled any trains that moved on that road in daylight. When we first went back to work it was several days before we were furnished with cloth tents, and during that time we had to look out for such quarters as we could find. So our fifty-six contingent prospected an old wood wagon shop, near by our brigade wagon yard. We found this old shop occupied by an old, dilapidated darkey—Uncle Tom—who was supporting himself by cobbling cooperage. After a survey of these premises we informed Uncle Tom that we had decided there was plenty of room for him and us, and we proposed to move in with him at once. While Uncle Tom did not seem at all flattered with our company, he did not openly protest, probably thinking it useless to do so. He said he could make out with one side if we could with the other side, with a common fire between on the ground, while there was a raised floor on each side. We also learned Uncle Tom had another lodger in the person of a young Georgia cracker who professed to belong to a pontoon corps. Uncle Tom had the appearance of being well raised—one of the old-time coloured gem-en, who had but little patience for po' white folks and especially soldiers of uncertain reputations. It was a cold, mid-January night when Uncle Tom got down his heavy comforts and made his bed. He had more cover than all of us, and a couple of us insisted that we sleep with him. But Uncle Tom drew the colour line on us and objected most emphatically to any such close relations. He said he was used to sleeping by himself and could rest better, besides, he was afraid of dem ar buggers. He was very careful about letting his bedding come in contact with our blankets. We were kind to Uncle Tom, and he soon became reconciled and quite sociable.

While here one day our Georgia cracker shouldered his gun and made a foray several miles up the south side of railroad in quest of pork or anything else to eat. He returned that evening with about a bushel of corn. He said he found some cars loaded with corn on a side-track and had broken in and helped himself.

He said, "As I come along up yonder I met General Lee. I saluted him as politely as I could, but he looked at me powerful hard, and I thought he was going to ask me where I got that corn, but he didn't. He was going out to where his big dam had broken loose, and was near where the canal was washed out. I stopped and watched him pass there, and he never looked out that way at all. I don't believe General Lee cares a damn about his big dam breaking and washing out the canal and railroad."

There were a few fat hens that ranged in our wagon yard. The next evening our cracker took a handful of his corn and passed innocent-like near a large, gentle hen, and dropping a few grains on into our shop quarters, the hen, following, was soon inside and the door was closed; and that hen failed to return home to roost. Uncle Tom was out at the time and never knew where that chicken came from.

The next morning, when Uncle Tom was shown how thick the grease was on the pot, he said, "That sho' is a fat chicken."

Then we told him if he had joined our mess and let us sleep with him he would have had a share in the chicken pot. He said he never did care a great deal about chicken any way. A few days later we got a good, new cloth tent and moved out and left Uncle Tom and his Georgia cracker alone. After the canal was mended, and we were running our boats, our cracker friend proposed to go up the river with us to forage for turnips; said if we would give him transportation he would divide the "catch" with us. After reaching the

61

woodpile and while we were loading he reconnoitred the neighbourhood and said he had located a healthy looking turnip patch; it was pretty close to the house, but thought he could raid it all right after dark. After supper the old man Baldwin, of the Twenty-fifth North Carolina, a rough-looking old mountaineer, who looked like he might have had experience in such raids in time of peace, said he would go with him, and they cheerfully set off. After they had been gone about an hour old man Baldwin came pulling in, puffing and blowing, and said "they put the dogs after us and shot at us. I didn't git but a handful and I dropped them as I got over the fence." Soon our cracker came in, looking like he was suffering a great bereavement, and when we laughed, he said, "I didn't think they would be so d—d particular about a few turnips this far out in the country." So we were all disappointed about our turnip soup. It would have been so nice with a few peppers. The navigation of the river was dangerous during high water. One night, while we were up in the second canal, the river rose several feet and was booming as we came out into it, and the strong current carried our boat against a drift on a small overflowed island, and came near sinking or capsizing it. Then the only way we could get off was down over a rough, shoaly slough, where she went like a bucking bronco. The next boat after us was manned by Alabamians, and they went over the lower rock dam that turned the water into the canal; being good swimmers, they got out, but lost their boat.

The 15th of March our Brigade was relieved from its position between the Appomattox River and the Norfolk railroad, where it had stayed continuously for nearly nine months, and moved about ten miles to the right on Hatch's Run. We came back to Petersburg and were in battle of Fort Steadman, in front of our old position, a sketch of which has been given.

Incidents On the Lines

The Yankees always showed a disposition to be friendly and wanted to talk to us, but our officers would not allow us to talk much, but had us to keep up a sharpshooters' fire on them all the while. However, we would occasionally exchange a few compliments. We used to inquire if they had any more Negroes they wanted buried; if they did, to blow out another hole and send them over and we would cover them up. One night, in front of the Twenty-fifth North Carolina Regiment, they changed their line, moving a section back a little. We inquired what they meant, and if they had an idea of leaving us. They replied, no, they expected to be neighbours for some time yet, but that the Twenty-fifth North Carolina was a little too close and was stealing their rations. The Twenty-fifth was a mountain regiment, every company west of the Blue Ridge, and was known in the brigade as the old roguish Twenty-fifth. It had a good fighting record.

One morning a large hawk came flying along between the lines. Both sides opened fire on it, and it became bewildered and lit on top of a tall poplar on City Point road, midway between the lines, and was soon shot out, both sides cheering and claiming it.

On March 25, after repelling a number of courageous assaults, our right falling back and being near a fort on our left, and assaulting columns pressing our front, we ceased firing to surrender. Our captors came up with flashing eyes and the loveliest smiles on their countenances and shook hands with us in the most enthusiastic manner. I could comprehend how good they felt when we ceased firing on them and they saw that they had gained a great victory. But as I passed through that fort, in and around where the dead of both sides lay thick, and saw a lot of freckle-faced Michigan boys vigorously firing on our men who were running back trying to get out, I felt like I wanted my gun again.

Then, as we were carried to the rear, the bullets from our side came singing over us and knocking up dust in the road, our guard said, "Run, Johnnie, run! Run, Johnnie, run!"

Our interest being the same, we were soon out of range.

Reminiscences of Point Lookout Prison

When we got there, the 27th of March, 1865, Negro troops guarded the outside walls and white men patrolled inside after night, and I saw nothing to criticise in the prison management; but those who had spent the winter there told some horrible and ludicrous stories of outrageous treatment by the Negro guard which, for awhile, guarded both outside and inside. A Negro guard would hear some one say, "Lay over or let me have some more cover."

If the Negro guard heard it he would say, "Who dat talking in dar. Send him out here quick or I'll make you all come out." Then, after double-quicking him around and making him mark time with his bare feet on the snow for a while, he would say, "Now pray for Abraham Lincoln. Now cuss Jeff. Davis. Now pray that some coloured gemmen may marry your sister—den I let you go back."

Some of these men said they could never die satisfied after they got out until they killed some Negroes on general principles.

A Negro Sergeant Who Claimed He Carried White Ladies' Hair

When I went out one day on a work detail I carried out to sell a watch chain made of the hair from a horse's tail or mane, and showed it to a Negro sergeant, who seemed to greatly admire its artistic beauty and inquired if the man who made it could make one of a lady's hair—that he wished to have one made from a lock of his sweetheart's hair that he possessed. I said I did not know; probably it would be too fine—when he answered, "It's no nigger wool; it's white lady har; my girl am a white lady." I answered, I don't know whether he can work it or not.

Begging Crumbs From a Negro's Table

One morning as I went out with the stable detail, as we were passing a Negro house, a six-year-old boy came to the door with a plate full of crumbs and crusts to throw out, when we asked him to give it to us. He gleefully held it out, while we rushed for it like hungry hogs. I got a handful. Then I thought; then I hesitated—subjugated, humiliated and degraded to begging the crumbs from a Negro's table. Then all the proud English, Irish and German blood in my veins rose up in protest, and I dashed it to the ground, though I was hungry enough to have licked all the plates in a whole Negro quarter.

Two Patriotic Soldiers and One Who Was Out For the Bounty

One day while working at the quarters of a German artillery company, located on the isthmus next the Potomac side, an American Yankee soldier came around and raised a friendly conversation about the war issues and boasted about how he had fought for the Union and how much longer he would fight. A Louisianan made issue with him and showed all the enthusiastic patriotism for the South. When they had exhausted their patriotic vocabularies the Yankee passed on, our German guard, a young, good-natured fellow, remarked to me, "I bees no war man; I does not want to fight."

Then I inquired how he came to be in the army, and he replied, "Oh, I bees a poor man; I has no money; they gives me three hundred dollars bounty, and I bees soldier." Then he remarked, "Our company all voted for McClellan; Lincoln loves the Nigger too much."

On the Wharf Detail and Wanting to Steal Something From Uncle Sam's Plentiful Stores

Several of us were in the big commissary prying around to get into the bean and potato barrels, when a wagon drove up and a Negro commanded us, saying, "Four you men go upstairs and bring down some cracker boxes and load dis wagon."

I got in the push and, as soon as we reached the cracker boxes we give a box a fling from the top of the pack and bursted it, when we all began eating like hogs. In a minute here came the Negro.

"What you-ens doin' dar? Dems our rations youse eatin'."

"A box fell and bursted, and we are gathering them up as fast as we can."

"Well, dat's all right, but don't you-ens eat no mo'."

"Can't we have these scraps."

"Yes, you may; you may have dem scraps."

We already had our pockets stuffed.

At another time, working around the commissary, I filled my pockets with beans and potatoes. These were the only full messes I got while in prison. The largest detail was known as the Fort detail, building and sodding a fort on the Potomac side. About three hundred men were worked on it. They got about three square inches or five cents worth of plug tobacco and a little drink of whiskey per day. The other details only give one pound of salt pork and a pint of vinegar for ten days' work. Working ten days for a pound of pork was rather low wages, but most of us were glad to get such an opportunity to get out. If we could pick up as much as the staves of a flour barrel we could sell it for ten or fifteen cents inside of prison, and a little money went a long way. Mackerel sold at five cents per pound, and a pound and a half loaf of bread for ten cents. The cheapest tobacco sold at one dollar per pound, and the men suffered as much for tobacco as for bread. The most of the users of tobacco would swap a piece of bread for a chew of tobacco. Tobacco retailed mostly by the chew. Tobacco was the most common medium of exchange. All of the smaller gambling concerns used pieces of tobacco cut up in chews, the larger cuts passing for five or ten chews. Rev. Morgan, the Confederate agent, conducted a school, which I attended some. Several preachers came in and preached to us, and the Catholic priests visited us occasionally, besides our local preachers held open air exercises frequently. The death of President Lincoln probably delayed our release. After the Confederacy went down we were aliens without government or protection in our native land. The proposition to take the oath of allegiance with full rights of citizenship under the old flag of our fathers seemed as good as we could expect, and we were soon anxious to do so and return home. About the 6th of June they began to discharge us. On the 11th of June the following was posted on the bulletin board:

All men whose homes are in Virginia and North Carolina who wish to return via Richmond, whose names begin with D and E, will be discharged upon taking the oath of allegiance to the United States on tomorrow—12th June.

So, before sunrise, I was on the front line of the penitents and on my knees awaiting for the blessing of being transformed from a rebel of the deepest dye into the marvellous light and liberty of a free, full-fledged, loyal American citizen—with all the privileges of a free "Nigger."

As one of the coloured soldiers had told me a few days before. He said, "De'l turn you out some dese days—den you'll be just as free as we is—and we is just as free as the birds."

The stars and stripes were stretched under the overhead ceiling of the school house; thirty-two of us stood under the flag that I had fired a thousand shots at, and, without mental reservation, took the oath and subscribed to the same in the records. I was marked, occupation, Planter (that sounded bigger than farmer); age, 19; eyes, blue; hair, auburn; complexion, fair; height, 6 feet 3¾ inches. I weighed 170 pounds when I went there, and got away with 145 pounds. We missed that day's ration and they gave us six hardtacks and a half pound of cod fish, which I eat at once. We (three hundred of us) arrived at Richmond after dark on the 13th of June. It was raining and we all held together and were instructed to report to the Provost office at capitol. As we marched the streets the ladies would remark, "Oh! look, there is our men; I am so glad to see them. Poor fellows, they are just out of prison."

The officer of the guard at the capitol informed us that no provision had been made for us, and advised us to go to the New Market for shelter and to report back at 9 a. m. Here we were furnished transportation—"free cars." This we took to the commissary and got rations. When we got to Richmond I had not eaten anything for more than thirty hours. A store keeper that night gave me two loaves of bread and some small fishes, dried herring, which was divided with my comrades, Virgil Elliott and Felix Dobbins. When Richmond was evacuated the people were destitute and most of them on the verge of starvation. So now the United States Government had nearly all of them to feed, white and black. When we went to get our rations two men drew together. I told my comrade to get our meat and I would get our bread. Avery, a consequential mulatto gentleman, waited on me, and when he weighed up my crackers, I said, "Meat for two men, please," and he throwed it up quick and pushed it to me. So I got a double ration of meat.

We crossed the James River on a pontoon bridge over to Manchester—all the bridges having been burned. Here we found many new freight cars marked U. S. M. R. R. We took up quarters in them to wait until 8 a. m. next day. That night a big rain broke down the road and we had to lay over another day. So I told Felix that I guessed more prisoners came in last night; let us go over and draw rations with them again, and he said all right. And we went over and drew another supply. I had now drawn eighteen pounds of salt pork to do me home. We sold the last draw to an Irish woman who kept a little shop, and we indulged in a quart of molasses. The people of Richmond were as clever and sympathetic with us as during the war. One storekeeper invited us to come in and help ourselves on sweet crackers (ginger snaps). The good lady that cooked our meat in Manchester sent with it a plate of nice, hot biscuits. We left Richmond June 16th, but our train could not cross the Appomattox River. The high water had careened the new trestle bridge. We walked over and on to another station, and a train from Burkville came after us. We stayed at Burkville until dark, and when we were ordered to board some box-cars, I found the door full, and they said not another could get in. I fought my way in and found those in the door all there were in it. So I hunted up my comrades,

Elliott and Dobbins, and brought them in, as a thunder storm was coming up. These men who tried to keep us out were hospital rats. They were clean and did not want to mix with us lousy, dirty prisoners. After we got in they let no others in, while many had to ride on top in an all-night rain storm. Thousands of Federal troops occupied Greensboro and Charlotte. They were all quite friendly and congratulated us on the close of the war. I said, "Well, you've freed the Negroes; now what are you going to do with them." They said, "Oh d—n the Niggers. I say kill 'em; they have been the cause of all this trouble." We had to walk home from Charlotte, sixty miles, and got home June 20th, very thankful that I was so fortunate to come back sound and well, while so many of my comrades had fallen by the wayside or were broken and maimed for life.

The Invasion of Home Land
After Lee's Surrender

Our section was never visited by an hostile army until some regiments of General Stoneman's cavalry passed from Rutherfordton to Lincolnton and back. They marauded the country in quest of horses and provisions. They scattered away from the main road and two came to my father's home. One held the horses and the other came in the house and said he wanted to search the house for arms, and soon went through bureaus, chests, etc. My mother's big, red chest had a double till in it with $10,000 of Confederate bonds and money in the lower till. The chest was full of bed clothes, and he felt under them, but did not find the Confederate money. Finding no valuables, the only thing he took from the house was the flint out of an old squirrel rifle.

A Faithful Negro Servant

All our good Negroes were true and faithful in helping to hide horses and other valuable property, but some mean Negroes would tell them where things were hidden, etc. My aunt, Mrs. Cabaniss, lived on the public road, and as Stoneman's men passed down they took a good mare out of the plough and carried it away. She only had two horses—the other was a blind mare. A week later they returned, going back towards Rutherfordton, followed by a drove of Negroes on foot. As they were passing Mrs. Cabaniss' a Negro saw her blind mare in the lot, bridled and rode it away. Her faithful old coloured servant, Edmond, saw the Negro riding the blind mare away, ran after them, appealing to the officers that they had taken the last horse and we will all perish. The officer told him to get his mare. He then procured a heavy stick and ran up beside the Negro and knocked him off, the troopers laughing and cheering him. He rode the blind mare back, and saved one horse to plough. Edmond remained faithful and stayed with his old miss as long as she lived, and he retained the confidence and good will of all the white people as long as he lived.

While Stoneman's troopers were raiding our section some of them called on Richard Smith, of Rutherford County, a good farmer and a good liver. He had a lot of nice bacon hams, and, expecting the raiders, he buried his hams in the house yard, fixed it up like a fresh grave and put up a headboard, marked Daniel. The troopers came, ransacked the premises and inquired about that grave in the yard. Smith told them that a faithful old servant had died a few days before, and his last request was to be buried in the yard, and, loving him so well, had complied. This explanation seemed to satisfy them, and they were about to leave, when one became sceptical and said, "Hold on boys, I think I would like to see Daniel before we go;" and, procuring a shovel, set in to raise him. Soon the dirt was cleaned off the box, then a plank was raised. He remarked, "Daniel looks natural; seems like I've seen him before somewhere. Well, boys, I guess we will take Daniel with us. Come out of here, Daniel, your country needs your services," and so they lifted him out.

Would Not Let Them Take All the Meat the Man Had

Amos Harrell, a good liver of the same county, tells how he saved his bacon. He hid it all out but three pieces. When the troopers came and raided his smoke-house an officer, looking in, ordered them out, saying, "You shall not take all the man's meat; leave him one piece." He locked the door and put the key in his pocket and carried it away.

Confederate Troopers Commit Outrages, Plunder and Murder

Joseph Biggerstaff, of Rutherford County, a farmer and country merchant, was visited by six Confederate troopers, who claimed to be Wheeler's men, on their way home. They demanded his money and, searching his house, found about $600 in *specie*. Four of them in the house put the money on a table to count it, while two men held the horses. Biggerstaff said he would die before they should take his money, but they paid no attention to him, when he attacked them with an axe, killing two and had the third one down when the fourth one at the table shot and killed him. There was present a man by the name of Waters, a neighbour, who had stood by and took no part. One of the robbers then upbraided Waters as a coward who ought to be killed, shot and killed Waters. Gathering up all the money, they left the four dead men where they had fallen, and rode away. This was the climax of the four years' bloody drama for our section. This last tragedy occurred near where a number of Tories were executed at Biggerstaff's old field, who had been taken at the battle of King's Mountain during the Revolutionary War. (See *Draper's History of King's Mountain and its Heroes*)

A Hearty Conscript

John Buncombe Crowder entered the army in 1863 as a 38-year-old conscript, and as a good family man had proved successful; but it was hardly expected that a man of his age should enter enthusiastically into the strenuous life of a soldier in times of great stress. However, John was inclined to hold up his end and made a faithful record. But the long, cold winter of 1865 in the trenches in front of Petersburg tired out his patience and he got powerful hungry. He stood six feet three inches and his fighting weight was 205 pounds. When we surrendered together, on the 25th of March, 1865, in front of Petersburg, Buncombe thought it good policy to make friends with his captors, in the hope of getting more and better rations; so he said, "Yes, I've quit fighting you. I've been wanting to quit for some time, and I shore am glad you've got me, for I am nearly starved to death

"Loss Bridges, the little man with the hot-gun, said, "He's lying to you, and at the same time showing a chunk of cornbread."

The Yankees said, "All right, Johnnie, you've got where there's plenty now, and you shall have plenty to eat."

B.: "Now I believe that I just know you'll treat me right."

Y.: "Ah, Johnnie, bet your life we will."

B.: "I've always thought you were clever fellows, and now I know it. I never did want to fight you nohow."

Y.: "Bully for you, Johnnie; you shall be taken good care of."

The men on the firing line who captured him would have done what they said; but prisoners are soon turned over to the bomb-proof brigade—coffee coolers and grafters—the kind of men who would get rich keeping the county poor-house. John Buncombe made a hard effort to get to the flesh pots and coffee cans of Yankeedom, but failed. He went up to Washington with the deserter volunteers, and was sent back to Point Lookout to starve with the rest of us. After he had been in a few days we asked him how he liked the fare, and he replied, "Very well; I don't have anything to do, and it don't take much to do me."

A few days more and he got so hungry he could hold his peace no longer and began to abuse the Yankees as the greatest liars and the meanest people in all the world, and he just wished he had held on to his gun and killed a few more of them anyhow. He had offered to go North and work for something to eat, and they would not let him, and were just holding to starve him to death for pure meanness. He said when he was at home it took a good-sized hen to make him a meal, and now we get nothing scarcely but bread, and he could eat four days' rations—two loaves or three pounds at one meal. So he raged and lectured as a champion eater until two men who had a little money got up a fifty-cent bet on him. He was to eat two loaves, or three pounds of bread, in thirty minutes.

A crowd gathered and much interest was manifested in the contest, and the eating began. In the excitement he took too much water. In ten minutes the first loaf disappeared and three canteens, or nine pints of water, with it. Then he said he did not have quite enough, but did not feel like he could eat all of the other loaf, so they need not cut it; that his stomach had shrunk up until he could not eat as much as he thought he could. After that he could no longer command a hearing, as his record as a champion eater was all he had to stand on. He is now—1907—living happily with his third wife and has plenty to eat, but says his appetite is not quite as good as it used to be.

Scenes at Appomattox—
Stragglers in the Union Army

Dr. Thomas L. Carson, my mother's youngest brother, who was in the Thirty-fourth North Carolina Regiment, Scale's Brigade, tells the following:

> We had stacked our muskets in surrender in the open beside the road, awaiting our paroles, when a large column of Federal troops passed us in steady, quiet tramp, followed by the rear guard bringing up about 2,000 stragglers. These stragglers wore a conglomeration of every trashy type to be found in the Yankee army. Foreigners of every tongue, mixed with every American type—old gray-headed men, beardless boys, big, greasy Negroes, etc., etc., all with battered and tattered clothing, some bareheaded and barefooted, and many without coats; some only had one pant leg on—all under a strong guard of peart-proud soldiers marching beside them with fixed bayonets. As they came along one big, stout fellow exclaimed, "Oh, yes, Johnnies; we've got you at last." A proud, peart-looking guard said, "Shut your mouth, you cowardly devil, or I'll pop my bayonet in you. You want to crow over these men. If many of our men had been like you, General Lee might now have had his headquarters in Boston instead of this surrender.

Dr. Carson says, as they started home, a young officer from Ohio walked along with him for half a mile and, talking of the situation, said:

"It looks very hard to start you men home without rations, but we are on short allowance ourselves, on account of your General Hampton, who cut down and destroyed eleven miles of our supply train a few days ago, or we would have had plenty to feed you on."

Once upon a time when the mulatto, Fred. Douglass, was orating, two Irishmen passing by stopped and listened a few minutes, then started on. One remarked, "He spaiks right well for a Nagur."

The other, "Oh, he's no Nagur; he is only a half Nagur."

"Oh, well then, if a half Nagur can talk that way, then I guess a whole Nagur could beat the prophit Jeremiah."

Once upon a time when North Carolina's last Afro-American Congressman—George White—was State Solicitor, a young Negro was on trial for some misdemeanour, and a white man was called upon to prove the defendant's character.

Solicitor: "Do you know this man?"

Witness: "Yes, sir."

"How long have you known him?"

"Oh, ever since he was a small boy."

"Well, sir; what is his character?"

"His character is good; good as any Niggers."

"Maybe you don't think a Negro has any character."

"Oh, I didn't say that."

"Now, sir; I ask you a direct question: Do you believe a Negro has got a character?"

"Oh, yes; he has a Nigger's character."

The Solicitor gritted his teeth and told the witness he could retire.

A Patriotic Darkey

While working outside on a detail at Point Lookout, a young coloured soldier, filled with patriotic enthusiasm, called on us and remarked:

"Hadn't been for us coloured troops I don't spec dese here Yankees ever would whipped you-uns."

"Did the coloured troops fight much?"

"Well, not 'zactly fitin'; but we do de gard duty so all de white soldiers could fight you, and den it seems like dey had all they could do."

An Aggrieved Union Soldier Seeks Sympathy From His Southern People

About the same time and place a young mulatto called on us and began to berate his comrades. He said, "Dese old, black Pennsylvania Niggers ain't got no sense nohow. Dey jest as mean as dey can be."

I said, "Ain't you a Pennsylvanian?"

"No, sir; I'se a Southerner, I is. I is a Virginian and I'se no kin to dem old, black Pennsylvania Niggers; but I'se some kin to you Southerners."

We told him we were sorry he had got into such bad company.

He said, "Yes, Southern folks heap the best."

A Southern railroad conductor said, "My Afro-American friend, you are in the wrong car; you must get in with your own colour."

"Well, Cap'n, if you say so, reckon I'll have to move; but what you goin' to do when we all gits to heaven?"

"Well, if I am conductor, you will move. Get along now."

A man travelling to West Virginia, where they have free cars, said as soon as they got out of Virginia, at the first stop, it was amusing to see the darkies vacate their cars and come piling into the white's coaches, thus showing how aggressive they are for social equality.

Field Officers of Fifty-Sixth Regiment North Carolina Troops

The field officers were all young, fine-looking men. Col. Paul F. Faison was tall, dark eyes, of the finest type of soldier, and we understood a West Point cadet. Lieut.-Col. Luke was about thirty years old, stout, medium size, sanguine temperament. Maj. John W. Graham, the son of an illustrious father, who served his State as Governor and United States Senator, William A. Graham. Major Graham, promoted from captain of Company D, was quite young, stout and hardy, always at his post except when disabled by wounds—full of youth and enthusiasm, he always proved himself the bravest of the brave. He is a prominent lawyer in his native town, Hillsboro. He has served as secretary of state and as state senator, and is one of the most prominent members of that body at session 1907. Maj. H. F. Schenck, who preceded Maj. Graham by one year's service, resigned on account of failure of health, and was assigned to service in the commissary department. Major Schenck is an affable gentleman of the highest type of citizen, a most useful and successful business man of his county, Cleveland. He is the promoter and manager of several cotton mills and a branch railroad. His chief partner is a Mr. Reynolds, of Philadelphia, Pa. Colonel Faison served in the interior department of the United States as Indian agent under President Cleveland's last administration. He died while in that service in Oklahoma Territory. Capt. Losson Harrell, M. D., of Company I, from Rutherford County, was senior captain and commanded the Fifty-sixth Regiment a part of the time during the siege of Petersburg. He has been for several years a member of the state board of health. Both Harrell and Schenck have also served as state legislators, and both are fine types of physical manhood.

All the captains were fine looking men, but we mention especially Captain Mills, of Company G, Henderson County, and Captain Alexander, Company K, Mecklenburg County—young, tall, and bravest of the brave. During the last week in May, 1864, in the breastworks at Bermuda Hundreds, on the morning that we took Gen. B. F. Butler's picket line and our dead and wounded were brought back, Capt. Alexander was standing in the midst of our company talking to our Captain Grigg, one of our young men, Thomas Nowlin, a gallant soldier and a cousin of mine, was seized with an epileptic fit, when Captain Alexander was the first to his assistance, and, kneeling over him, did everything he could for him. If he had been one of his own men or even a brother he could not have shown more sympathetic interest. This greatly impressed me as to the real character of the man, and verified the adage, "the bravest are the tenderest." I was greatly hurt a few weeks later when this noble young officer fell in battle. I think about the 20th of August, on the Weldon railroad. He was of the sanguine temperament of the Scotch-Irish type.

Our captain, B. F. Grigg, had a wife and baby that he thought more of than of the Confederacy after hope of success was on the wane. He held out faithful to the end, but was so glad when the cruel war was over that he turned Republican and was for many years postmaster at Lincolnton and a successful merchant. He went in early—joined

First Regiment of six months' volunteers—and was in first battle at Bethel, Va.; but he got enough by and by, and wanted to quit.

Brigadier-General Matt. W. Ransom, our Brigade Commander, is too well known to the people of this country to require an extended introduction by me, he having served twenty-four years in the United States Senate and four years as minister to Mexico. All who have known him recognize in him the highest type of the old-time southern Christian gentleman. As an officer he held the deserved love and highest respect of all his men. He was scholarly, gentle, sympathetic, and a most pleasant and entertaining orator. He would go anywhere in the state to address his old soldiers, always giving them the most patriotic advice. He was an enthusiastic optimist on the great resources and possibilities of our great united country. The last time he addressed the Confederate veterans of Shelby, N. C., about two years before he died, money was raised and tendered him to pay his expenses, when he said, "No! no! I can not take the boys' money; I don't need it, and if I did I could not take it."

Among the younger officers none excelled General Hoke, of Lincolnton, N. C. He entered the army as a company officer at less than twenty-four years of age. He was soon colonel of the Twenty-first North Carolina Regiment, then brigadier-general. He had not handled a brigade long until General Lee witnessed one of his gallant and most successful assaults and rode out of his way to compliment him personally, and there is no doubt, as the sequel will show, but that General Lee ever after held him in his highest confidence. He was with Stonewall Jackson in all his most brilliant campaigns. After his gallant brigade had been worn to a frazzle following Gettysburg, he was sent back to North Carolina to rest and recruit. After a few months of comparative rest, he boarded a train at Weldon, N. C., and went to Richmond to President Davis and presented a campaign for eastern North Carolina, upon the completion of the gun-boat, *Albemarle*, nearing completion at Halifax, N. C., stating that he thought with two brigades beside his own that he could take Plymouth, Washington and New Bern, N. C., and thus clear his state of all its invaders. President Davis heard him patiently and then said he was glad to hear someone who still thought something could be done, and said he would transfer some ranking officers and give him the forces suggested. This writer got these facts from his uncle, Gen. John F. Hoke. General Pickett had made an expedition against New Bern February 1, 1864, with six brigades, and could easily have taken it had not some of his plans miscarried. An account of General Hoke's taking Plymouth and Washington and his service at Drury's Bluff and at Cold Harbor are given in a former chapter. General Hoke was sent back to North Carolina and commanded at Wilmington, N. C., finally surrendering with General Johnson. General Hoke is very modest about exploiting his brilliant military career; but we have it on the authority of the *Charlotte Observer* that during the last months of the war General Lee became apprehensive that his health might give way at any time, and looking over the whole field, selected General Hoke to take his place as his successor, and had such an understanding with President Davis and General Hoke. At the beginning of the Spanish-American War, we heard that President McKinley offered General Hoke a brigadiership, and he modestly declined it. The writer met General Hoke twenty-five years after the war, and upon complimenting his brilliant campaigns, as an actor and eye-witness, he said, "Yes, when I had to fight them I tried to go at it so as to make them think I was not afraid of them." He said he was not quite twenty-eight years old when the war closed. General Hoke is an uncle to Governor Hoke Smith, of Georgia. Besides being with General Hoke in his Eastern North Carolina and Drury's Bluff campaigns, I got most of my information from Capt. L. E. Powers, now of Rutherfordton, N. C., who served with General Hoke first in the Twenty-first North Carolina Regiment and then in his brigade, and under him through four years. Captain Powers has represented his county three terms in the legislature. He says he has been under fire with General Hoke in about forty engagements and was wounded several times.

A True Virginia Boy and
a Bit of Romance

While this writer was located on the canal, boating wood for the men in the trenches at Petersburg, winter of 1865, he became acquainted with a widow lady, Mrs. Dean, and family of three children; a grown daughter, Miss Jennie, and a younger daughter, Miss Lucy, aged about twelve, and a little son, aged about ten years. They occupied a neat cottage near his quarters. They were a nice, intelligent family, then in deep mourning for a son and brother, the hope and mainstay of the family, who had fallen in battle a few months before. Young Dean had proved so good a soldier and had so distinguished himself for personal bravery from all the battles through the Wilderness on down to Petersburg, that his officers had given him a sixty day furlough to stay with his mother. When he had been at home a few weeks, keeping in touch with his regiment, which was on the lines of defence near by, in August, when the Federals seized the Weldon Railroad and a desperate battle was expected, he kissed his mother and sisters and hastened to join his regiment, and went into battle that day and shed his life's blood that day in defence of his native city, his home and loved ones, proving himself one of the greatest heroes in Lee's invincible army of battle-scarred veterans. What nobler deed! What greater sacrifice can any people

show? Our relations with this good family became recip-
rocal. They would do some cooking for us, and we would
bring them some wood. I guessed Miss Jennie was about
my age, nineteen, medium in size, blue eyes, dark hair, most
lovely form and features, of an honest, sincere expression.
For all that is good and lovely in woman, she filled my ideal;
but pleasant associations are soon broken in war, and I was
ordered to report to my regiment. I had a supply of rations
from home and Miss Jennie made me some cakes of sor-
ghum molasses, and we parted, hoping to meet again soon
and to correspond sure. My command moved ten miles
to the right on Hatches' Run for ten days; then back past
Miss Jennie's home in the night, and on into the battle in
front of Petersburg on the 25th of March. Here I threw up
the "sponge" and went to Point Lookout and stayed there
until the 12th June; then came back by Richmond, and
on home. We had no mails for a year after the war, before
I wrote Miss Jennie that I had got through in good shape.
Then she wrote me a nice letter, informing me that she
had married a young Confederate soldier—a Mr. Jones—
and giving a cordial invitation to visit them if I ever came
to Petersburg. Well, as time pulled on, I, too, was married
in 1872, and was as happy as any one could be. Forty years
after parting with Miss Jennie I concluded to visit Petersburg and the old battlefields. I was now a grandpap and a
widower, and I thought of my old friend, Mrs. Jones, and I
wondered what had become of them. If she and her husband were living, I would certainly give them a call. Then,
if I should find her a widow, there might be a little bit of
new romance started in the Old Dominion. I could think
of her only as the lovely girl of nineteen; but I had to reflect
that she, too, might now be a withered grandmother. I went
on the Seaboard Road and landed right in our old wagon
yard. The beautiful oak grove was all gone, streets and hun-

dreds of houses covered our old stamping ground. I soon located the old canal, like unto a sunken road, and could recognize only the old brick mill house at the lower end of the canal basin or boat landing. Seeing some old veterans around I inquired if they knew Mrs. Dean, and they said they did, and Jennie too. That she married Ned Jones; that Jones had been dead a couple of years.

Then I enquired, "How is Mrs. Jones?"

"She is an invalid—not able to get out. A son and a daughter live with her."

"What sort of a man was Jones?"

"He was a good man, a local preacher. She lives second block—third house on the right."

Starting out to see my poor invalid lady friend, I stepped in where beer was sold and got a glass. I then interrogated the proprietor, Mr. Quarles. He said he was raised there, was about sixteen at close of the war; had served with the old men and boys; had stood in the breastworks and helped repel several attacks upon Petersburg. Yes, he knew Mrs. Dean and her family well. Then he told the pathetic story of the death of young Dean, and said he came very near going with him into that battle. That Miss Jennie married Lewellyn Jones, a brother of Ned Jones; that they moved to Crews, Va. Then I learned from him and others that Miss Jennie had been dead thirty years, leaving no children, and her husband had remarried and had a family of grown children; and that Miss Jennie's little brother lived in the city, the last of the family living. Then I took a street car for the Crater, where I had laboured and fought forty years before, and after taking in the museum of war relics, went out where I had thrown some lead, and in an oat stubble picked up some battered bullets. A pine tree large enough for a saw log is growing in the bottom of the Crater, since the 1,500 skeletons had been removed to national cemeteries.

Col. Billy Miller's
Upright Farm. . . .

This famous county, the place of my nativity as well
as that of many others of more or less national and local
prominence, such as Thomas Dixon, Jr., of the Clansman
fame; Hon. E. Yates Webb, Congressman Ninth District;
Col. A. M. Lattimore, of Lattimore; Capt. O. D. Price, the
old-time singer; Capt. Pink Petty, the famous fox-hunter
with the silver-mounted horn; Capt. Nim Champion, the
standing candidate for the legislature on the one-plank
platform—the restoration of the whipping-post. Then we
have Frank Barrett, the old soldier candidate, who always
runs on just any platform the people want, and who distinguished himself during the Civil War by going up in a
balloon over the enemy for a pint of whiskey, with many
others too tedious to mention, such as bankers, cotton mill
men and shop keepers, etc. This goodly heritage lies east
of the Blue Ridge and is flanked by the South Mountains
on the north, Cherry Mountains encircling the west, with
the famous little King's Mountain on the south. One large
township embraces the South Mountains.

Little First Broad River with numerous tributaries, flows

from these mountains south, making a diversified, rolling country, interspersed with hills and sandy flats. There was a man in our company, F, in the Confederate army from the mountain section of our good county by the name of John Wesley Richards, a stalwart fellow of thirty, who for three years was a brave and courageous soldier; but after lying in the bloody trenches of Petersburg eight and one-half months, during which time he was wounded, he became disheartened and, forsaking all rights and interest in the Confederacy, shouldered his musket and, taking a dozen of his comrades with him, set out to fight his way home, and were successful in reaching home about the time General Lee surrendered, so they were not molested. Besides the right to hold Negro slaves, there was another right dearer to the people of upper Cleveland, *viz*, the right to convert their sour apples into brandy and their corn into whiskey, infringed upon by the Yankee government. After the surviving remnants of the Confederate army came home, and the shirkers came in from the bushes, all of the little copper stills started up for a joyful time, and public sentiment was so strongly against Federal interference that they were not molested much for two or three years. Our hero, John Wesley Richards, after his long, arduous campaigns in the war, felt that he was entitled to a season of rest and recreation, with plenty of refreshments thrown in to boot. So he got on a long and continuous spree, and went to the bad, until his wife had to divorce him and turn him out to "root hog or die." Then, after a while, he began to rally and reform; and a grand, speculative idea striking him, he traded his faithful squirrel dog and his old shot gun for a warrantee deed for one hundred acres of land in the upright region of Cleveland County. Then, as Wesley began to prosper, he found himself in need of a one-horse wagon, called in these parts a "carryall"; and learning that J. S. Groves, a big merchant at Shelby, kept wagons to sell for cash and on time, Wesley wended his way to Shelby and, looking over Mr. Groves' wagons, said he would like to have the running works of a one-horse wagon, but did not have the cash to pay down. Mr. Groves said that was all right; if he could give him a good paper he could have the wagon. John Wesley said he could give him a mortgage on one hundred acres of land. Mr. Groves said that would do. The papers were fixed up, the wagon delivered and John Wesley went on his way home rejoicing. The next fall Mr. Groves notified him that his note was due and they would expect him down soon to settle. A few weeks later he wrote Wesley that if he did not come soon and make some arrangements that he would have to advertise that land. John Wesley heeded not these warnings, and the land was advertised; and here is where Col. Billy Miller butted in and bought a cheap farm. Col. Billy had served in the cavalry during the war and managed to pull through in good shape. After engaging in several enterprises he founded a weekly newspaper called *The Shelby Aurora*, and made a great success. So this was the paper the land was advertised in. When the land was sold, lying twenty-five miles from town, none of the town people knew anything of it. Colonel Billy started it at forty cents per acre, which covered the cost of the wagon and advertisement, and no one bettered it, and he thought he had picked up a great bargain. Now this writer used to be somewhat connected with the *Aurora*. When his crops were short and prices low he could always get a job with Colonel Miller during the winter months to help out making ends meet, collecting and drumming up new subscribers. The *Aurora* was very popular—good coarse print so everybody could read it—and most everybody took it whether they could read or not. Its chief policy was to flatter all its patrons—those who paid for it because they paid and those who did not pay in hopes they would pay. When a man re-covered his house, built a new stable or cleared a fresh field we called him one of our most industrious and enterprising citizens, and when a fellow came to town to buy a side of bacon or a sack of flour on time he was alluded to as being on a business trip; and when nothing else good could be said of a fellow, we would puff him on his enthusiastic and steadfast Democracy. The way to run a county paper is to brag on all the people all the time and keep a good list of subscribers, and the patent medicine fellows will pay the running expense. So one winter, as I was ranging around the mountains near Colonel Miller's farm, I met up with Blacksmith George Towry, a jovial, good-natured man, who said, "Tell Miller to send me his paper six months for showing those fellows his farm and trying so hard to sell it to them."

He sent two young men up here and referred them to me and I went over there and showed it to them and bragged on it all I could. When we got to the house I said, "You see that large white-oak on the lower side of the yard, that is the place to have your hog pen; it will always produce acorns enough to fatten a hog; then see that large hickory in front of the house; it is full of squirrels every day in the fall, and while your hog is fattening you can sit in the door and shoot a mess as you need them. Then, if you get tired eating squirrels, just look out yonder in that old field at the simmon trees. They are full of 'possoms every night, and you can gather a mess as you need them. Then when you kill your hog and get tired of so much greasy doings, just go up on the side of the mountain and cut some gum logs and you can catch all the rabbits you want. Don't you see its the easiest place to live you ever saw? Then look down there at that spring, as pure water as ever come out of the ground; it would be worth a thousand dollars anywhere in Texas; and the climate can't be beat anywhere in the world—malaria, microbes and such things never bother us. These high mountains on the north and east break off the cold winds. In winter you can set out on a log in the sunshine all day and enjoy the scenery; then, if you are ambitious and enterprising, you could start up a turkey ranch right here; you have sixty thousand acres of free range, enough to raise 10,000 turkeys, with at least fifty cents per head net profit; that gives you $5,000 per year income on turkeys alone. I tell you that would beat raising cotton on the sandy flats all hollow. All the expense raising turkeys would just be to throw them a little corn to keep them gentle. The young men looked puzzled and one said, 'And where would we get the corn?' 'Oh,' said I, 'you could find some corn down at Jack Morrison's mill or at Ped Price's store.' Then one says, 'And how could we get the turkeys to market?' and I says, 'Oh, drive them out; they can fly across these deep hollows.' He then added, 'The young men turned away looking sorrowful, and I don't know whether they will buy or not.'"

Uncle Abe Wallis Visits Washington

A few years ago a story was current of an old darkey from Salisbury, N. C., visiting Washington, D. C., to see the President and obtain social recognition. We name him. Uncle Abe Wallis was an industrious, well-behaved matter-of-fact old darkey who had accumulated the snug sum of forty dollars, and concluded to spend it in the advancement of his social position, and he reasoned that the shortest way to get to the top quick would be to call on the President for recognition. So he paid $15.00 for a ticket and boarded a flyer, and was on his way to the Mecca of Afro-American hopes, rights and social privileges, looking disdainfully upon the common blacks as he sped by them along the way, he was soon in the city of equal rights for all with special privileges for none. After being relieved of two dollars for a night's lodging at a coloured hotel, bright and early he inquired the way and set out for the White House, where he expected to take dinner and wanted his name in the pot in time. When he had had an insight of the coveted goal and turned in that direction, he was accosted by a harsh voice, "Whar ye goin'?"

"Well, sar; I'se on my way to visit the President."

"This is not the day to see the President."

"Well, I don't care anything about your arrangements; but this is my day to see him."

"I guess not."

"Captain, call the wagon and give this man a ride."

"Den, befo' I could parley any mo' about it, dey chucked me in de wagin and went down one of dem wide roads as hard as dey could tare and soon turned up at a 'spectable enough looking buildin'. Den dey tell me to git out, and when I go in dey feel in my pockets and take my money and say, 'Guess we better save dis, de bums will clean you up.' Den dar I was with a passel of no count looking Niggers and some po' drunken white trash—about de worst company I ever got into. Next mornin' de Jedge call me out and ax what my name and where I live. I say my name am Abraham Wallis and my home are Salisbury, N. C. Den he say, 'What is your business,' and I tell him I am a deacon in our Baptist church. Den he say, 'And what is your business here?' an' I tell him I come specially to visit the President and let him know that there was as good an' 'spectable coloured people in North Carolina as dere was in Alabama. Den he say, 'Old man, I'll discharge you on condition that you take the first train South; you can't afford to circulate around here; someone will pull your *wad* and you will be stranded along way from home. Go home while you can'; and soon I was comin' back just as fast as I went. I tell ye I'se seen 'nough of Washington; de coloured man haint got no showin' at all. At Raleigh I can jest walk right into the Governor's office and nobody'll say, 'Where you gwine?' And de Governor would say he felt pleased to see me, and he'd give me my dinner too; but he wouldn't eat with me. I'se hearn about dis yaller Nigger, Booker Washington, who goes up North to eat wid white folks. He runs a big school and a big farm down in Alabama and gits all de young coloured boys he can to go to school some and to work on his farm lots; and he tells 'em dey ought to be powerful glad to get to work on de farm, while he sends his own children off to Wesley University, in school wid white children. Take it all round, the honest coloured person is respected about as much in North Carolina as anywhere, and I 'spect to stay at home after dis and keep on good terms wid our white folks, for dey is the best after all."

An Irish Socialist

Patrick Finnegan had been studying socialism and told his friend, Barney O'Brien, that socialism was a good thing, both charitable and Christian, and if the people would adopt it all would be prosperous and happy.

Barney says, "Pat, if ye had two homes, would ye give me one?"

"To be sure I would," says Pat.

"Then if ye had two horses, would ye give me one?"

"Then certainly I would," says Pat.

"Then if ye had two hogs would ye give me one?"

"No. To hell with ye, Barney; ye know I've got thim."

"Well, that was what I was thinking, that ye would hold to your pigs with all the tenacity that a Vanderbilt would grip his railroads. It is aisy enough to give away what ye ain't got; but if ye can't practice what ye preach ye had as well shut up."

"Now that's just like ye, Barney; ye would never make a good socialist. Ye would rob me entirely. You know I need me hogs; but I would not need but one home, and one horse would be all I could work and feed."

"Yes, Pat, and I guess if ye wait until ye get a home and a horse you'll be a socialist a good while yet."

"To be sure I will, and if you ever have a home at all it will be when I have one to give you."

Barney: "Then I guess I had better hold my job and not depend on ye."

Pat: "Along with ye, Barney; it may be well that ye can always find a boss."

Seven Days' Fight Around Richmond

Reminiscences of Dr. Alexander, of Charlotte, N. C., recall to me the scenes of those battle-fields of the seven days' battles of McClellan, 1862, when we passed over the ground in June, 1864, on our way to the Chickahominy River. Many of the Federal dead had scarcely been buried at all, as the rank weeds over the naked bones and blue rotten uniforms showed, where groups of a score or more had been bunched in shallow graves and lightly covered.

Out of the 2,700 soldiers furnished the Southern army by Mecklenburg, how few remain to tell of that fearful seven-days' struggle. The weather had been intensely hot before the fighting began for several days. Many of our men were on the sick list. On the 25th inst. the long roll was sounded; our troops, the Thirty-seventh Regiment, was hastily formed in line. Confederate battle-flags were here first displayed; stretchers for bearing off the wounded were here first put in charge of the ambulance corps. Everything wore a death-like hue. John Bell, a member of my company, said he was not able for the march, was sick; I spoke to the surgeon, and told him I would take Bell's word for anything. He said, "Leave him behind."

In a week he was dead. Another fellow asked me

to intercede for him, that he was sick. I told him I knew Bell, but I could not vouch for him; when night came he deserted, and is living yet. This was as we were leaving camp at Brock Church, six miles north of Richmond. We camped near Meadow Bridge. On the 28th we moved slowly down the Chickahominy; got on the edge of the road to let a body of Yankee prisoners pass; one of our men asked them where they were going; an Irishman answered, 'In faith, I am going to Richmond, where me wife has been telling me to go for the last two months, and how far is it yit?'

Late in the afternoon we heard heavy cannonading in our front, and we pushed forward rapidly, bearing to the left, as we thought, to charge a battery. Shells were passing through our line, killing seven men in one company; when we got in thirty steps of the battery we were ordered to lay down, to support the battery. The artillery duel ceased about 8 o'clock, and remained quiet until 9 o'clock next morning, when it broke loose with a vengeance and was quickly over. General Jackson had got in McClellan's rear. Here the sun was terribly hot as we lay on the southern slope of the hillside, with nothing to protect us from the vertical rays of the sun. We went from here to Mechanicsville, where the heavy fighting was done the evening before. Here the Yankee dead had not been moved, and the swarms of horse-flies that arose from the dead carcasses rendered it necessary for each man to hold one hand over his mouth and nose. It is impossible to describe the scene as it was. In the afternoon of the 27th we reached Gains' Mill; this battle opened about 3 p. m. It was terrific. North Carolina's loss was very great.

It was here that Colonel Campbell was killed. Capt. Billy Kerr was desperately wounded. Many private soldiers and company officers from Mecklenburg were killed and wounded. A rare sight I witnessed. Some man, I never knew who he was, was riding back and forth in front of our firing line, talking to the men, telling them to aim low, don't shoot too high; he was bareheaded, wounded in the neck; no coat on, and was riding a gray horse; the blood had run down from his neck to his gray horse; he appeared cool and determined. A large and spotted hound appeared at the same time, running and barking as heavy limbs were cut off by shells, licking the blood from the dead and wounded. I don't know what became of the dog or the man on horseback.

When the battle was over, I was appointed to the medical department and assigned to the Thirty-seventh Regiment. We went next to the bloody field of Frazier's farm. Here our colonel, Charles C. Lee, was killed; he was as gallant an officer as ever trod the battle-fields of Virginia; he was as brave as a lion and gentle as a lamb, and thought it not inconsistent with his profession as a soldier, to acknowledge Jesus Christ as the captain of his salvation.

The next move was to overtake McClelland's army, which was halted at Malvern Hill. Here General McGruder was in front, and his orders were to feel what position the enemy occupied. It was said at the time that McGruder was so pleased with the position of his artillery that he at once *'let slip the dogs of war.'* This proved the bloodiest battle of the war for the time it lasted. From personal observation I can testify that there was no break in the roar of musketry for five hours. The gunboats on the James

River threw large shells at random, most of which burst over their own troops. The battle closed at 10 o'clock at night. Immediately the Yankee army sought the shelter of their gunboats. It took us two days to get the wounded all off to Richmond. One peculiar case of gun-shot wound I will mention. A soldier by the name of Rankin, Company H, Thirty-seventh Regiment, shot in the base of the skull of the *medulla oblongatta*, did not prevent him from walking about; was examined by a dozen surgeons, but were unable to trace or locate the bullet, when Dr. Campbell, of the Seventh Regiment, called me as the youngest surgeon to try my hand. In a jest I placed my hand on his forehead and told him to open his mouth; at once I saw a swelling in the roof of his mouth; it was hard and smooth. I made a slit with a scalpel, and showed a minnie ball to the astonished surgeons. How the ball got there without killing him has always been a mystery.

President Davis spent a night with us; he was in fine spirits, but seemed deeply touched at the sight of so much suffering. We passed by the battle-ground two days after the battle; the field was rolling; our dead were all buried; it looked like a thousand-acre field of potato hills. The enemy were still lying where they fell. They must have fought with great desperation, as their line of battle was plainly to be seen by about every third man being killed. This line could be traced one mile and a half.

After waiting a few days to rest, and the enemy showing no disposition to renew the fight, our men, from privates to general officers, began a general hunt for them pesky little fellows that are not known in polite circles. I have seen five hundred men have their shirts off at one time, looking for—what they were sure to find. After this campaign we had a great deal of typhoid fever; the hospitals being full of wounded, the most of the cases were treated in camp, more successfully than they would have been in Richmond hospitals. *Lest we forget.*

The Negro Problem

Say what you will, it is the cause of all the sectional prejudice and hatred ever engendered in this country. Thousands
of millions of money and hundreds of thousands of lives of
good white men have been sacrificed in the solution of the
Negro problem for this country, and still it hangs over us
the darkest cloud that obscures the bright vision of peace
and good will to all men. And as the biologists say, "He
stands out in his dark isolation a perpetual challenge to the
dogma of the unity of the races."

We understand him as a slave. In that capacity he filled
every expectation that could be required of him, always
reflecting the character of his master. If the master was
very religious, so was he. If the master was a drunkard and
a sinner, so was he. Always a good imitator, but never an
originator. He liked to be flattered and honoured and was
always faithful to every special trust. When kindly treated
he loved his master like a child. These were the conditions
that the discipline of slavery obtained. Now his status has
changed and all personal restraints are removed and strict
discipline stopped. He is now thrown upon his own resources, and must stand upon his own merits. He is now
inclined to neglect the patient, hard-earned virtues of the
whites, and to imitate their easy vices. He is handicapped at
every turn by race prejudices. The professions in most places are closed to him. He is not wanted anywhere except as

a cheap hewer of wood and drawer of water. All intelligent white labour resent his competition, even in the humblest work. White lawyers and doctors get some pickings out of him, and where he is numerous white merchants have a good pull on him. All who are getting anything out of him are willing to tolerate him. All who get nothing out of him would gladly see him deported. Wherever he gets a foothold in country or city he depreciates real estate by making conditions more or less intolerable. He is a prolific subject for religious fanatics and cranks to practice upon. He is an alien here in his native country among his own people. He is the only man in all the world ashamed of himself and his colour. His greatest ambition is to be evoluted into a white man, and he wants to start right now, and so long as that boon is denied him will he be an aggressive alien. Since the old masters and old servants have passed away there is no friendship or kind interest between their descendants, and the gulf is widening all the while. This great country, leading the vanguard of civilization for all the world, must do justice to all men. Now what can we do with the Negro? Shall we keep him here a standing menace and a perpetual challenge to mob law, and increase our police force, or deport him and sustain a strictly white man's country. If we deport him as fast as Europeans come in, we would soon be done with him as a factor in politics and labour; but as yet we have no place to send him. Through industrial and commercial relations we will soon absorb Mexico and the Central American States, and upon the completion of the Panama Canal we can expand rapidly into South America, where there is a vast area of unsettled country that would make an ideal Negro country—throughout all of the Amazon River country territory could be procured for the colonization of all our Negroes under the fostering care of the United States, where the black man may hold all the offices and fulfil all the functions of complete citizen-ship, with close commercial relations in the exchange of products. I have been taxed forty years for freeing him, and would consent to be taxed forty years more to remove him to such a paradise as herein suggested.

We want the Chinese excluded because they are too docile and carry a head of their own. Then we want the Jap excluded because he is too smart for us to compete with. When we lose a few million white men fighting Japan, as we will have to do soon, as they swarm over here, dictating how they shall be treated, then the white man's burden will be pretty heavy with the coloured problem, and a general house-cleaning may follow that will purify the political at-mosphere somewhat.

In the meantime all of our great, soulless corporations, transportation and manufacturing companies regard all "coons alike," whether they be white, black, yellow, brown or ring-streaked or striped. They exploit them for what profit there is in them without regard to the interest of the present or future generations. What did it matter to the Pharaohs what was to be the future of their country, so long as they had plenty of slaves to rear gigantic pyramids to their own selfish ambition.

In peace or war, where is the town that would have Ne-gro troops quartered in it, for fear at any time they be of-fended, shoot up the town and massacre the women and children? Anywhere in this country that the Negro is de-nied full social rights, he stands offended and ready to enact any tragedy that promises to advance his social position. The whites must decide whether they shall warm him in their bosoms or cast him off. Nothing has ever been more firmly implanted in the human breast than race prejudice. No first-class white man can feel at ease on social equality with the coloured races.

LEONAUR

ALSO FROM LEONAUR
AVAILABLE IN SOFTCOVER OR HARDCOVER WITH DUST JACKET

JOURNALS OF ROBERT ROGERS OF THE RANGERS *by Robert Rogers*—The exploits of Rogers & the Rangers in his own words during 1755-1761 in the French & Indian War.

GALLOPING GUNS *by James Young*—The Experiences of an Officer of the Bengal Horse Artillery During the Second Maratha War 1804-1805.

GORDON *by Demetrius Charles Boulger*—The Career of Gordon of Khartoum.

THE BATTLE OF NEW ORLEANS *by Zachary F. Smith*—The final major engagement of the War of 1812.

THE TWO WARS OF MRS DUBERLY *by Frances Isabella Duberly*—An Intrepid Victorian Lady's Experience of the Crimea and Indian Mutiny.

WITH THE GUARDS' BRIGADE DURING THE BOER WAR *by Edward P. Lowry*—On Campaign from Bloemfontein to Koomati Poort and Back.

THE REBELLIOUS DUCHESS *by Paul F. S. Dermoncourt*—The Adventures of the Duchess of Berri and Her Attempt to Overthrow French Monarchy.

MEN OF THE MUTINY *by John Tulloch Nash & Henry Metcalfe*—Two Accounts of the Great Indian Mutiny of 1857: Fighting with the Bengal Yeomanry Cavalry & Private Metcalfe at Lucknow.

CAMPAIGN IN THE CRIMEA *by George Shuldham Peard*—The Recollections of an Officer of the 20th Regiment of Foot.

WITHIN SEBASTOPOL *by K. Hodasevich*—A Narrative of the Campaign in the Crimea, and of the Events of the Siege.

WITH THE CAVALRY TO AFGHANISTAN *by William Taylor*—The Experiences of a Trooper of H. M. 4th Light Dragoons During the First Afghan War.

THE CAWNPORE MAN *by Mowbray Thompson*—A First Hand Account of the Siege and Massacre During the Indian Mutiny By One of Four Survivors.

BRIGADE COMMANDER: AFGHANISTAN *by Henry Brooke*—The Journal of the Commander of the 2nd Infantry Brigade, Kandahar Field Force During the Second Afghan War.

BANCROFT OF THE BENGAL HORSE ARTILLERY *by N. W. Bancroft*—An Account of the First Sikh War 1845-1846.

LEONAUR

ALSO FROM LEONAUR
AVAILABLE IN SOFTCOVER OR HARDCOVER WITH DUST JACKET

AFGHANISTAN: THE BELEAGUERED BRIGADE *by G. R. Gleig*—An Account of Sale's Brigade During the First Afghan War.

IN THE RANKS OF THE C. I. V *by Erskine Childers*—With the City Imperial Volunteer Battery (Honourable Artillery Company) in the Second Boer War.

THE BENGAL NATIVE ARMY *by F. G. Cardew*—An Invaluable Reference Resource.

THE 7TH (QUEEN'S OWN) HUSSARS: Volume 4—1688-1914 *by C. R. B. Barrett*—Uniforms, Equipment, Weapons, Traditions, the Services of Notable Officers and Men & the Appendices to All Volumes—Volume 4: 1688-1914.

THE SWORD OF THE CROWN *by Eric W. Sheppard*—A History of the British Army to 1914.

THE 7TH (QUEEN'S OWN) HUSSARS: Volume 3—1818-1914 *by C. R. B. Barrett*—On Campaign During the Canadian Rebellion, the Indian Mutiny, the Sudan, Matabeleland, Mashonaland and the Boer War Volume 3: 1818-1914.

THE KHARTOUM CAMPAIGN *by Bennet Burleigh*—A Special Correspondent's View of the Reconquest of the Sudan by British and Egyptian Forces under Kitchener—1898.

EL PUCHERO *by Richard McSherry*—The Letters of a Surgeon of Volunteers During Scott's Campaign of the American-Mexican War 1847-1848.

RIFLEMAN SAHIB *by E. Maude*—The Recollections of an Officer of the Bombay Rifles During the Southern Mahratta Campaign, Second Sikh War, Persian Campaign and Indian Mutiny.

THE KING'S HUSSAR *by Edwin Mole*—The Recollections of a 14th (King's) Hussar During the Victorian Era.

JOHN COMPANY'S CAVALRYMAN *by William Johnson*—The Experiences of a British Soldier in the Crimea, the Persian Campaign and the Indian Mutiny.

COLENSO & DURNFORD'S ZULU WAR *by Frances E. Colenso & Edward Durnford*—The first and possibly the most important history of the Zulu War.

U. S. DRAGOON *by Samuel E. Chamberlain*—Experiences in the Mexican War 1846-48 and on the South Western Frontier.

LEONAUR

ALSO FROM LEONAUR
AVAILABLE IN SOFTCOVER OR HARDCOVER WITH DUST JACKET

OFFICERS & GENTLEMEN *by Peter Hawker & William Graham*—Two Accounts of British Officers During the Peninsula War: Officer of Light Dragoons by Peter Hawker & Campaign in Portugal and Spain by William Graham .

THE WALCHEREN EXPEDITION *by Anonymous*—The Experiences of a British Officer of the 81st Regt. During the Campaign in the Low Countries of 1809.

LADIES OF WATERLOO *by Charlotte A. Eaton, Magdalene de Lancey & Juana Smith*—The Experiences of Three Women During the Campaign of 1815: Waterloo Days by Charlotte A. Eaton, A Week at Waterloo by Magdalene de Lancey & Juana's Story by Juana Smith.

JOURNAL OF AN OFFICER IN THE KING'S GERMAN LEGION *by John Frederick Hering*—Recollections of Campaigning During the Napoleonic Wars.

JOURNAL OF AN ARMY SURGEON IN THE PENINSULAR WAR *by Charles Boutflower*—The Recollections of a British Army Medical Man on Campaign During the Napoleonic Wars.

ON CAMPAIGN WITH MOORE AND WELLINGTON *by Anthony Hamilton*—The Experiences of a Soldier of the 43rd Regiment During the Peninsular War.

THE ROAD TO AUSTERLITZ *by R. G. Burton*—Napoleon's Campaign of 1805.

SOLDIERS OF NAPOLEON *by A. J. Doisy De Villargennes & Arthur Chuquet*—The Experiences of the Men of the French First Empire: Under the Eagles by A. J. Doisy De Villargennes & Voices of 1812 by Arthur Chuquet .

INVASION OF FRANCE, 1814 *by F. W. O. Maycock*—The Final Battles of the Napoleonic First Empire.

LEIPZIG—A CONFLICT OF TITANS *by Frederic Shoberl*—A Personal Experience of the 'Battle of the Nations' During the Napoleonic Wars, October 14th-19th, 1813.

SLASHERS *by Charles Cadell*—The Campaigns of the 28th Regiment of Foot During the Napoleonic Wars by a Serving Officer.

BATTLE IMPERIAL *by Charles William Vane*—The Campaigns in Germany & France for the Defeat of Napoleon 1813-1814.

SWIFT & BOLD *by Gibbes Rigaud*—The 60th Rifles During the Peninsula War.

LEONAUR

ALSO FROM LEONAUR
AVAILABLE IN SOFTCOVER OR HARDCOVER WITH DUST JACKET

BUGEAUD: A PACK WITH A BATON *by Thomas Robert Bugeaud*—The Early Campaigns of a Soldier of Napoleon's Army Who Would Become a Marshal of France.

WATERLOO RECOLLECTIONS *by Frederick Llewellyn*—Rare First Hand Accounts, Letters, Reports and Retellings from the Campaign of 1815.

SERGEANT NICOL *by Daniel Nicol*—The Experiences of a Gordon Highlander During the Napoleonic Wars in Egypt, the Peninsula and France.

THE JENA CAMPAIGN: 1806 *by F. N. Maude*—The Twin Battles of Jena & Auerstadt Between Napoleon's French and the Prussian Army.

PRIVATE O'NEIL *by Charles O'Neil*—The recollections of an Irish Rogue of H. M. 28th Regt.—The Slashers—during the Peninsula & Waterloo campaigns of the Napoleonic war.

ROYAL HIGHLANDER *by James Anton*—A soldier of H.M 42nd (Royal) Highlanders during the Peninsular, South of France & Waterloo Campaigns of the Napoleonic Wars.

CAPTAIN BLAZE *by Elzéar Blaze*—Life in Napoleons Army.

LEJEUNE VOLUME 1 *by Louis-François Lejeune*—The Napoleonic Wars through the Experiences of an Officer on Berthier's Staff.

LEJEUNE VOLUME 2 *by Louis-François Lejeune*—The Napoleonic Wars through the Experiences of an Officer on Berthier's Staff.

CAPTAIN COIGNET *by Jean-Roch Coignet*—A Soldier of Napoleon's Imperial Guard from the Italian Campaign to Russia and Waterloo.

FUSILIER COOPER *by John S. Cooper*—Experiences in the 7th (Royal) Fusiliers During the Peninsular Campaign of the Napoleonic Wars and the American Campaign to New Orleans.

FIGHTING NAPOLEON'S EMPIRE *by Joseph Anderson*—The Campaigns of a British Infantryman in Italy, Egypt, the Peninsular & the West Indies During the Napoleonic Wars.

CHASSEUR BARRES *by Jean-Baptiste Barres*—The experiences of a French Infantryman of the Imperial Guard at Austerlitz, Jena, Eylau, Friedland, in the Peninsular, Lutzen, Bautzen, Zinnwald and Hanau during the Napoleonic Wars.

LEONAUR

ALSO FROM LEONAUR

AVAILABLE IN SOFTCOVER OR HARDCOVER WITH DUST JACKET

CAPTAIN COIGNET *by Jean-Roch Coignet*—A Soldier of Napoleon's Imperial Guard from the Italian Campaign to Russia and Waterloo.

HUSSAR ROCCA *by Albert Jean Michel de Rocca*—A French cavalry officer's experiences of the Napoleonic Wars and his views on the Peninsular Campaigns against the Spanish, British And Guerilla Armies.

MARINES TO 95TH (RIFLES) *by Thomas Fernyhough*—The military experiences of Robert Fernyhough during the Napoleonic Wars.

LIGHT BOB *by Robert Blakeney*—The experiences of a young officer in H.M 28th & 36th regiments of the British Infantry during the Peninsular Campaign of the Napoleonic Wars 1804 - 1814.

WITH WELLINGTON'S LIGHT CAVALRY *by William Tomkinson*—The Experiences of an officer of the 16th Light Dragoons in the Peninsular and Waterloo campaigns of the Napoleonic Wars.

SERGEANT BOURGOGNE *by Adrien Bourgogne*—With Napoleon's Imperial Guard in the Russian Campaign and on the Retreat from Moscow 1812 - 13.

SURTEES OF THE 95TH (RIFLES) *by William Surtees*—A Soldier of the 95th (Rifles) in the Peninsular campaign of the Napoleonic Wars.

SWORDS OF HONOUR *by Henry Newbolt & Stanley L. Wood*—The Careers of Six Outstanding Officers from the Napoleonic Wars, the Wars for India and the American Civil War.

ENSIGN BELL IN THE PENINSULAR WAR *by George Bell*—The Experiences of a young British Soldier of the 34th Regiment 'The Cumberland Gentlemen' in the Napoleonic wars.

HUSSAR IN WINTER *by Alexander Gordon*—A British Cavalry Officer during the retreat to Corunna in the Peninsular campaign of the Napoleonic Wars.

THE COMPLEAT RIFLEMAN HARRIS *by Benjamin Harris as told to and transcribed by Captain Henry Curling, 52nd Regt. of Foot*—The adventures of a soldier of the 95th (Rifles) during the Peninsular Campaign of the Napoleonic Wars.

THE ADVENTURES OF A LIGHT DRAGOON *by George Farmer & G.R. Gleig*—A cavalryman during the Peninsular & Waterloo Campaigns, in captivity & at the siege of Bhurtpore, India.

LEONAUR

ALSO FROM LEONAUR
AVAILABLE IN SOFTCOVER OR HARDCOVER WITH DUST JACKET

THE LIFE OF THE REAL BRIGADIER GERARD VOLUME 1—THE YOUNG HUSSAR 1782-1807 *by Jean-Baptiste De Marbot*—A French Cavalryman Of the Napoleonic Wars at Marengo, Austerlitz, Jena, Eylau & Friedland.

THE LIFE OF THE REAL BRIGADIER GERARD VOLUME 2—IMPERIAL AIDE-DE-CAMP 1807-1811 *by Jean-Baptiste De Marbot*—A French Cavalryman of the Napoleonic Wars at Saragossa, Landshut, Eckmuhl, Ratisbon, Aspern-Essling, Wagram, Busaco & Torres Vedras.

THE LIFE OF THE REAL BRIGADIER GERARD VOLUME 3—COLONEL OF CHASSEURS 1811-1815 *by Jean-Baptiste De Marbot*—A French Cavalryman in the retreat from Moscow, Lutzen, Bautzen, Katzbach, Leipzig, Hanau & Waterloo.

THE INDIAN WAR OF 1864 *by Eugene Ware*—The Experiences of a Young Officer of the 7th Iowa Cavalry on the Western Frontier During the Civil War.

THE MARCH OF DESTINY *by Charles E. Young & V. Devinny*—Dangers of the Trail in 1865 by Charles E. Young & The Story of a Pioneer by V. Devinny, two Accounts of Early Emigrants to Colorado.

CROSSING THE PLAINS *by William Audley Maxwell*—A First Hand Narrative of the Early Pioneer Trail to California in 1857.

CHIEF OF SCOUTS *by William F. Drannan*—A Pilot to Emigrant and Government Trains, Across the Plains of the Western Frontier.

THIRTY-ONE YEARS ON THE PLAINS AND IN THE MOUNTAINS *by William F. Drannan*—William Drannan was born to be a pioneer, hunter, trapper and wagon train guide during the momentous days of the Great American West.

THE INDIAN WARS VOLUNTEER *by William Thompson*—Recollections of the Conflict Against the Snakes, Shoshone, Bannocks, Modocs and Other Native Tribes of the American North West.

THE 4TH TENNESSEE CAVALRY *by George B. Guild*—The Services of Smith's Regiment of Confederate Cavalry by One of its Officers.

COLONEL WORTHINGTON'S SHILOH *by T. Worthington*—The Tennessee Campaign, 1862, by an Officer of the Ohio Volunteers.

FOUR YEARS IN THE SADDLE *by W. L. Curry*—The History of the First Regiment Ohio Volunteer Cavalry in the American Civil War.

LEONAUR

ALSO FROM LEONAUR
AVAILABLE IN SOFTCOVER OR HARDCOVER WITH DUST JACKET

THE RELUCTANT REBEL by William G. Stevenson—A young Kentuckian's experiences in the Confederate Infantry & Cavalry during the American Civil War..

BOOTS AND SADDLES by Elizabeth B. Custer—The experiences of General Custer's Wife on the Western Plains.

FANNIE BEERS' CIVIL WAR by Fannie A. Beers—A Confederate Lady's Experiences of Nursing During the Campaigns & Battles of the American Civil War.

LADY SALE'S AFGHANISTAN by Florentia Sale—An Indomitable Victorian Lady's Account of the Retreat from Kabul During the First Afghan War.

THE TWO WARS OF MRS DUBERLY by Frances Isabella Duberly—An Intrepid Victorian Lady's Experience of the Crimea and Indian Mutiny.

THE REBELLIOUS DUCHESS by Paul F. S. Dermoncourt—The Adventures of the Duchess of Berri and Her Attempt to Overthrow French Monarchy.

LADIES OF WATERLOO by Charlotte A. Eaton, Magdalene de Lancey & Juana Smith—The Experiences of Three Women During the Campaign of 1815: Waterloo Days by Charlotte A. Eaton, A Week at Waterloo by Magdalene de Lancey & Juana's Story by Juana Smith.

TWO YEARS BEFORE THE MAST by Richard Henry Dana. Jr.—The account of one young man's experiences serving on board a sailing brig—the Penelope—bound for California, between the years1834-36.

A SAILOR OF KING GEORGE by Frederick Hoffman—From Midshipman to Captain—Recollections of War at Sea in the Napoleonic Age 1793-1815.

LORDS OF THE SEA by A. T. Mahan—Great Captains of the Royal Navy During the Age of Sail.

COGGESHALL'S VOYAGES: VOLUME 1 by George Coggeshall—The Recollections of an American Schooner Captain.

COGGESHALL'S VOYAGES: VOLUME 2 by George Coggeshall—The Recollections of an American Schooner Captain.

TWILIGHT OF EMPIRE by Sir Thomas Ussher & Sir George Cockburn—Two accounts of Napoleon's Journeys in Exile to Elba and St. Helena: Narrative of Events by Sir Thomas Ussher & Napoleon's Last Voyage: Extract of a diary by Sir George Cockburn.

LEONAUR

ALSO FROM LEONAUR
AVAILABLE IN SOFTCOVER OR HARDCOVER WITH DUST JACKET

IRON TIMES WITH THE GUARDS *by An O. E. (G. P. A. Fildes)*—The Experiences of an Officer of the Coldstream Guards on the Western Front During the First World War.

THE GREAT WAR IN THE MIDDLE EAST: 1 *by W. T. Massey*—The Desert Campaigns & How Jerusalem Was Won---two classic accounts in one volume.

THE GREAT WAR IN THE MIDDLE EAST: 2 *by W. T. Massey*—Allenby's Final Triumph.

SMITH-DORRIEN *by Horace Smith-Dorrien*—Isandlwhana to the Great War.

1914 *by Sir John French*—The Early Campaigns of the Great War by the British Commander.

GRENADIER *by E. R. M. Fryer*—The Recollections of an Officer of the Grenadier Guards throughout the Great War on the Western Front.

BATTLE, CAPTURE & ESCAPE *by George Pearson*—The Experiences of a Canadian Light Infantryman During the Great War.

DIGGERS AT WAR *by R. Hugh Knyvett & G. P. Cuttriss*—"Over There" With the Australians by R. Hugh Knyvett and Over the Top With the Third Australian Division by G. P. Cuttriss. Accounts of Australians During the Great War in the Middle East, at Gallipoli and on the Western Front.

HEAVY FIGHTING BEFORE US *by George Brenton Laurie*—The Letters of an Officer of the Royal Irish Rifles on the Western Front During the Great War.

THE CAMELIERS *by Oliver Hogue*—A Classic Account of the Australians of the Imperial Camel Corps During the First World War in the Middle East.

RED DUST *by Donald Black*—A Classic Account of Australian Light Horsemen in Palestine During the First World War.

THE LEAN, BROWN MEN *by Angus Buchanan*—Experiences in East Africa During the Great War with the 25th Royal Fusiliers—the Legion of Frontiersmen.

THE NIGERIAN REGIMENT IN EAST AFRICA *by W. D. Downes*—On Campaign During the Great War 1916-1918.

THE 'DIE-HARDS' IN SIBERIA *by John Ward*—With the Middlesex Regiment Against the Bolsheviks 1918-19.

www.ingramcontent.com/pod-product-compliance
Lightning Source LLC
Chambersburg PA
CBHW031856090426
42741CB00005B/525